Living & Working in Saudi Arabia

Living & Working in Saudi Arabia

*Your guide to a successful
short or long-term stay*

ROSALIE RAYBURN
2nd edition

How To Books

Published by How To Books Ltd,
3 Newtec Place, Magdalen Road,
Oxford OX4 1RE. United Kingdom.
Tel: (01865) 793806. Fax: (01865) 248780.
email: info@howtobooks.co.uk
www.howtobooks.co.uk

First edition 1997
Second edition 2001

British Library Cataloguing in Publication Data
A catalogue record for this book is available from
the British Library

Cartoons by Mike Flanagan
Cover design by Shireen Nathoo Design
Cover image PhotoDisc

Produced for How To Books by Deer Park Productions
Typeset by PDQ Typesetting, Newcastle-under-Lyme, Staffs.
Printed and bound by The Cromwell Press, Trowbridge,
Wiltshire

NOTE: The material contained in this book is set out in good
faith for general guidance and no liability can be accepted
for loss or expense incurred as a result of relying in particular
circumstances on statements made in the book. Laws and
regulations are complex and liable to change, and readers should
check the current position with the relevant authorities before
making personal arrangements.

Contents

List of Illustrations

Preface
to the Second Edition

The Kingdom of Saudi Arabia is a country of mysteries and rapid change where time-honoured customs and traditions exist side by side with the latest technological developments. For every aspect of daily life there is a public face and a private face. Even if you have spent time in other parts of the Middle East, Saudi Arabia is a unique experience which requires numerous adjustments. This book has been written to provide businessmen and professionals, their wives and families, with practical up-to-date information which will help them acclimatise to a culture which is very different from anything they have experienced before. Especially valuable is a chapter specifically addressing the changes that women face in adapting to life in the Kingdom.

Throughout the book the words 'Westerners', 'expatriates' and 'expats' have been used as generic terms to describe overseas employees, principally from Europe and North America. This is the term commonly used by people living in the Kingdom. Since there is no standard spelling for Arabic words in English, all Arabic words used in the text are rendered strictly phonetically.

Living and Working in Saudi Arabia provides essential information on practical matters such as visa requirements, housing, school and health concerns. It also lists numerous commercial and government contacts, which make it a valuable reference tool for the business person. Widespread Internet access is relatively new to Saudi Arabia and this edition provides information which will enable the reader to conduct further research online.

I would like to thank Rosemary Scott and Jennifer Leighty for their valuable assistance in updating this book.

Rosalie Rayburn

1

Introducing Saudi Arabia

THE COUNTRY AND ITS REGIONS

Saudi Arabia is the largest country on the Arabian Peninsula, located between the Red Sea and the Arabian (also known as the Persian) Gulf. It covers an area of 2.2 million square miles, half the size of continental Europe. There are not only the vast deserts and date palm oases of popular legend, but steep mountains and cool green valleys. The Western Province (Al Hejaz), along the Red Sea, has the major port city of Jeddah and the holy cities of Mecca and Medina. Several hours' drive north of Jeddah is the industrial city of Yanbu which has a relatively large expatriate population.

Jeddah is the most cosmopolitan city in Saudi Arabia. It was the traditional port of entry for Muslims from all over the world on their obligatory pilgrimage to Mecca. The Hejaz was under Turkish rule from the 16th century until King Abdul Aziz took control in 1925. The present day Kingdom owes its existence to Abdul Aziz Ibn Abdul Rahman Al Saud. In the first three decades of the 20th century Abdul Aziz (also referred to as Ibn Saud) swept across the country conquering and winning the allegiance of scattered tribes. Until the mid-1980s Jeddah was the diplomatic capital of Saudi Arabia. Only then did all the foreign embassies move to the Diplomatic Quarter in the capital, Riyadh. There are still several foreign consulates, including a British Consulate, in Jeddah.

In the heart of Jeddah is the historic Al Balad district which is a protected area. Many of the old houses have been restored as they were a century ago and are open to tourists. More modern development has taken place along the waterfront known as the *Corniche*. There are numerous fountains and statues and it is a popular place for family picnics.

The Muslim holy city of Mecca (also spelled Makkah) is about 70 km east of Jeddah. This is where the Prophet Mohammed was born in AD 570. Mecca is Islam's holiest city and the pilgrimage (*hajj*) to Mecca is one of the five obligations of every Muslim. At the centre

Fig. 1. Map of Middle East showing Saudi Arabia and neighbouring countries.

of the city is the grand Mosque and the sacred ZamZam Well. The *Kaaba*, at the centre of the Grand Mosque is the focal point to which Muslims worldwide turn when they pray.

The Prophet Mohammed began preaching in his native Mecca but due to local opposition he fled to nearby Medina (also spelled Madinah). The date of his flight in AD 622 is counted as the beginning of the Islamic, or *Hejira* calendar which operates throughout the Arab world. The most important place in Medina is the Prophet's Mosque which contains his burial place. Mecca and Medina are off-limits to non-Muslims and there are tightly controlled checkpoints on all roads leading to the cities. The Medina airport and Medina Sheraton Hotel are, however, open to non-Muslims.

To the north of Medina are the archaeological ruins of Madain Salah which rival the better known ancient city of Petra in neighbouring Jordan. The vast stone tombs of Madain Salah were carved between 100 BC and AD 100. Both cities were built by the Nabateans whose empire thrived through controlling the important incense caravan route between southern Arabia and Syria to the north.

In the mountains near Jeddah and Mecca is the city of Taif. Its altitudes and cool pleasant climate makes it an attractive summer resort for families from Jeddah and Riyadh.

To the south, the Southwestern Province has the mountainous area known as the Asir. Until 1922 when it was conquered by King Abdul Aziz, Asir was an independent kingdom with close ties to neighbouring Yemen. The cool rainy climate of Asir make it the only area of the Kingdom where life is comfortable without air conditioning. The main cities in Asir are Abha and Najran. The latter has a fort which has some beautiful examples of traditionally carved doors and windows.

In the Central Province (Al Najd) is the capital city, Riyadh and the ancestral home of the Al Saud family. It is also the largest province extending from the great Nafud desert bordering Jordan and Iraq to the vast Empty Quarter (Rub Al Khali) in the south bordering the United Arab Emirates (UAE) and Oman. North of Riyadh are the towns of Buraidah, Unaizah and Ha'il. This is the most traditional area of the country and the most religiously conservative. Few Westerners travel into this region and the town of Buraidah is the only place in Saudi Arabia where even foreign women must wear veils.

Most of the capital city of Riyadh has been built within the last twenty to thirty years. Since the mid-1980s all government ministries and embassies have been located there. Of historical interest is the Mismak fort which Abdul Aziz (later King Abdul Aziz) captured in 1902. Abdul Aziz eventually became Emir or ruler of the Najd and later established his rule over the whole area now known as Saudi Arabia by 1932. King Abdul Aziz built the Murabba Palace in 1946 and this is now the official home of the present Saudi ruler King Fahd.

Dirya, outside Riyadh, was the capital of the first Saudi state when the Al Saud family held power during the 18th century. It has been restored and is open to tourists.

The Eastern Province (Al Hasa) borders the Arabian (also known as the Persian) Gulf. Al Hasa is the centre of the oil industry with numerous production fields and one of the largest refineries in the world on the Arabian Gulf at Ras Tanura north of Dammam. In 1933 King Abdul Aziz granted the first oil concession to Standard Oil of California (SOCAL). Oil was first discovered near the coastal city of Dammam in 1938. In 1944 a group of oil companies: SOCAL, Texas Oil Company (Texaco), Standard Oil of New Jersey (EXXON) and Socony Vacuum (MOBIL), formed the Arabian American Oil Co. (ARAMCO).

ARAMCO located its operation in what is now called Dhahran. The nearby fishing village of Al Khobar grew rapidly and is now home to many thousands of expatriates working in the oil and related industries. In 1980 the 25 km King Fahd causeway was completed making it possible to drive to the neighbouring island of Bahrain which is a popular weekend getaway.

Dammam is the administrative capital of the Eastern Province but remains more traditional than Dhahran or Al Khobar. To the north is the industrial city of Jubail where a number of petrochemical plants are located.

The town of Hofuf, about two hours' drive inland from Al Khobar, is in the centre of the country's largest oasis. Its historic fort and outdoor market (*souq*) are well worth a visit. Also of historic interest in the Eastern Province are the town of Qatif and nearby islands of Tarut and Darin just north of Dammam. You can visit the Thursday morning market in Qatif and explore the remains of a Portuguese fort on Tarut.

Introducing Saudi Arabia's population

In 1999 the Saudi Arabian population was estimated at 20.5 million. Of that number over 5 million are expatriates. The majority of these are men from all over Asia, working on single status contracts. The number of Europeans and Americans is much smaller. Since oil was discovered in its Eastern Province in 1938 Saudi Arabia has developed at an astonishing rate. From being a land of wandering Bedouin tribes, and isolated trading and oasis settlements, Saudi Arabia of today boasts modern cities connected by super-highways, hospitals offering high-tech health care and a universal education system.

Tales of fabulous wealth abound, but due to the very private nature of the culture it is rare to see much evidence of ostentatious lifestyles. Wealthy Saudis may build large, elaborate houses, but they are always behind substantial walls. While there are many fine buildings in the major cities, for the most part the numerous three- and four-storey apartment blocks of the Saudi towns are uniformly beige and undistinguished. Everyone tends to drive fast but flashy cars are a rare sight. The most popular vehicles are the huge GM Suburbans, suited to transporting large families, and large, white Chevrolets which boast powerful air conditioning systems.

The country's neighbours
Saudi Arabia's immediate neighbours are Jordan, Iraq, Kuwait, Yemen, the United Arab Emirates, Oman, Bahrain and Qatar.

WHAT IS THE CLIMATE LIKE?

For Europeans familiar with temperate climes and, at best, Mediterranean summer holidays, Saudi Arabia is unbelievably hot. From April to October temperatures are over 35°C daily throughout most of the country, while during July, August and early September they are often 40 to 45°C.

Regional variations
In the Western Province, along the Red Sea coast, cities such as Jeddah and Yanbu are humid and sticky during the hot months, while in Riyadh and inland desert areas it is both hotter and drier in summer and cooler in winter.

The coastal towns of the Eastern Province, Dammam, Al Khobar and Jubail, have mixed humid and dry weather during the hot season, and usually enjoy some rain between December and March.

In the southern part of the Western Province, in the mountainous Asir region near the Yemen, border towns like Abha and Khamis Mushayt enjoy much cooler summers and winters.

Since rain is relatively infrequent, perhaps 2.5 inches a year in Jeddah, up to 7 inches in the Asir region and around 3 inches a year on the east coast, the result is often flooded streets in the towns and flash-floods in the desert. Although it is hot throughout the Kingdom from mid-May to mid-October, the remainder of the year is mild and pleasant during the day, with cool to cold nights.

PRACTICAL INFORMATION

The Kingdom

The official name is the Kingdom of Saudi Arabia, *Al Mamlaka Al-Arabia Al-Saudia*. The Kingdom is divided into fourteen provinces governed by *Emirs* (Governors) appointed by the king.

King Abdul Aziz Ibn Abdul Rahman Ibn Saud united the country during the first three decades of the 20th century. He died in 1953 leaving 43 sons and numerous daughters. He has been succeeded by the following of his sons:

Saud 1953–1964
Faisal 1964–1975
Khalid 1975–1982
Fahd 1982–present.

The government

Monarchy
King Fahd, known as The Custodian of the Two Holy Mosques, is head of the state and Prime Minister. However he is now basically retired.

Crown Prince
Abdullah, brother of King Fahd, Deputy Prime Minister and Commander of the National Guard. Crown Prince Abdullah is now in charge of all day-to-day governing.

Second Deputy Prime Minister
Also Minister of Defence and Aviation, and Inspector General: Prince Sultan, brother of King Fahd.

Council of Ministers
Appointed by the king.

Consultative Council
Majlis Ash-Shura, set up in 1992. The sixty members of the Council are appointed by the king. The Council has no legislative powers and its recommendations are not binding.

Majlis
Sessions at which the king, crown prince and governors hear petitions from citizens and expatriates.

Ulema
A group of religious scholars who regulate religious life in Saudi Arabia.

Constitution
The Holy Qu'ran.

System of law
Shari'a (Islamic law).

Religion
Islam: the majority of Saudis belong to the main Sunni sect. A minority group of Shiia Muslims is concentrated in the Eastern Province. The split between Sunnis and Shiites stems from a dispute over who should be the true successor of the Prophet Mohammed.

Official language
The official language of Saudi Arabia is Arabic. Due to the Kingdom's long association with Great Britain and the US the Saudis are well versed in the English language.

Currency
Saudi Riyal: 100 halalahs = 1 SR.
   Notes are available in 1, 5, 10, 20, 50, 100, 200 and 500 denominations. The exchange rate is currently SR 5.75 = £1.00 sterling. (Check for fluctuations.)

Time difference from UK
Saudi Arabia is three hours ahead of GMT, or two hours ahead of GMT during British Summer Time (April to October).

Scheduling your working week
Saturday to Wednesday or Thursday; Friday is a day of rest.

Business hours

Shops:	Sat – Thurs: 8.30 or 9 am until midday prayer, reopening 4 – 9.30 pm (varies in small towns).
Banks:	Sat – Thurs: 9 am – 1.00 pm and 3 – 5 pm.
Government offices:	Sat – Wed: 7.30 am – 2.30 pm.
Other businesses:	Sat – Thurs: 8 am – 1 pm and 4 – 7 pm.

Prayer time closing

All shops must close during the daily prayer times (*Selah*). As these times change very slightly each day, a schedule of prayer times for major cities in the Kingdom is published daily in the three English language newspapers. (See Fig. 11, page 97).

Ramadan

During the Holy Month of *Ramadan* all Muslims are required to fast from dawn to dusk (see Living with Islam below) and are only allowed to work six hours a day. Shop and business hours during this period vary significantly from the rest of the year. Businesses are usually open from 9 am to 3 pm and from 8.30 pm to midnight. Banks are open from 9 am to 1 pm and 8 pm to 11 pm.

This is only a rough guide, as hours do vary from place to place during *Ramadan*.

Cash and credit cards

Although many Saudis still make purchases on a cash basis, most stores accept credit cards. Many shops add on a credit card handling fee. The fee should be no more than three per cent of your purchase.

Using banks

The banks offer extensive services and it is easy to open an account. Most people open an account with the bank which serves their company. You may choose to shop around for the bank which offers services that meet your needs. Below is a list of services compiled from various banks.

- Current account: for depositing and withdrawing cash.

- Savings account: under Islamic law interest rates are forbidden, but you do receive a 'commission' from the bank. Shop around for the best commission.

- Travellers' cheques.

- Credit cards: many banks have their own credit cards and have set up discount agreements with retailers so shoppers receive discounts when using their cards.

- Automatic teller machines (ATM): ATM cards are offered and ATM machines are located throughout the country.

- Paying utility bills: an invaluable service for expats living off-compound.

- Transfer of funds: both in the Kingdom and abroad.

- Accounts can be in Saudi Riyals and/or pounds sterling.

- Foreign currency exchange service.

- Cheque cashing: if at the bank the cheque is drawn on, it is cashed immediately. Cashing a cheque from a different bank will take approximately three days, and the funds can then be transferred to your account automatically.

Posting mail

It is common to have all your post sent to your company's post office box address. Mail from the UK usually takes seven to ten days, occasionally up to fourteen days. Parcels sent air mail take seven to ten days, but it is not unusual for parcels to take a few months to reach you due to custom's inspection. Post offices are located centrally in the large cities, but there are very few post boxes. Individuals frequently have mail posted from their workplace and pay the charge. Postage to the UK is SR 4.50 for letters up to 50 g. For urgent items DHL courier service is available, but it is very expensive. It is worthwhile bringing UK stamps with you, as friends or colleagues going back to the UK on leave will post mail for you.

Other postal rates are as follows:

Letters – non-Arab countries
1–10 g SR 2; 20–50 g SR 3; 50–100 g SR 7; 250–500 g SR 15

Printed non-Arab countries
1–50 g SR 3; 50–100 g SR 4; 100–250 g SR 9;

Small parcels non-Arab countries
1–100 g SR 6; 100–250 g SR 13;150–500 g SR 23

Registered
SR 4 and over.

All mail (letters as well as packages) is subject to censorship. Remind your friends and relatives not to send any prohibited materials. You will be the one who suffers the consequence of your friends' indiscretion, which could result in a prison sentence or deportation.

Making international calls

Offices and private villas or apartments have direct telephone lines. International calls can be dialled direct. Faxes can also be sent from home computers or fax machines. It can sometimes be difficult receiving faxes at a home extension.

Most **compounds**, however, have a switchboard-type telephone system. Each resident is at an extension. When calling someone at a compound number the call will either be answered by a gate guard, who will put you through to the extension, or sometimes there is a pre-recorded message such as 'Welcome to XYZ Compound, please dial your extension during this message or wait for operator assistance'. If you have a touch tone telephone you will be able to dial the extension. Otherwise the call will roll back to the gate guard.

To make international calls, dial 00 followed by the country code, then the area code minus the first zero, then the number. For example, to call a London number dial 00 44 0207 or 0208 then the number. The international code for Saudi Arabia is 966.

Some area codes in Saudi Arabia

Abha	07	Khamis Mushayt	07
Abqaiq	03	Khafji	03
Buraidah	06	Kharj	01
Dammam	03	Khobar	03
Dhahran	03	Mecca	02
Hafr-al-Batin	03	Ras Tanura	03
Hofuf	03	Tabuk	04
Jeddah	02	Taif	02
Jubail	03	Yanbu	04

International directory assistance	900
Directory assistance	905

The cost of international calls
Calls from Saudi Arabia to UK cost SR 8 per minute (approx £1.39). There is a twenty per cent reduction from 11 pm to 3 am, and forty per cent discount from 3 am to 9 am. Calls from UK to Saudi Arabia cost 72p per minute.

LIVING WITH ISLAM

Islam is one of the three major religions in the world which originated in the Middle East. It is the religion of the majority of the people throughout the entire Gulf area, as well as North Africa, much of Asia and Indonesia. Islam is based on the revelations of the word of God (Allah) as delivered to the Prophet Mohammed, which are written down in the Holy Book known as the *Qur'an*, and the sayings of the Prophet known as the *Hadith*. The *Qur'an* is accepted as the direct work of God and is therefore considered infallible. Even translations from the original classical Arabic into other languages are not considered valid.

Islam, which means, submission to the will of God (Allah), is often described as a way of life. All Muslims learn the *Qur'an* from an early age. The *Qur'an* contains comprehensive guidelines on every aspect of daily life. Certainly it is *the* way of life in Saudi Arabia. Islam governs the political, legal and social life of everyone in the country. Anyone who will be visiting, working or living in Saudi Arabia should read as much as possible about Islam in order to understand the motivation behind the attitudes and values of the country (see Further Reading).

The Five Pillars of Islam
The basic tenets of Islam are as follows:

- Monotheism: 'There is no God but Allah and Mohammed is His Prophet'.

- Prayers: all Muslims must pray at five set times each day.

- Fasting: Muslims must fast from dawn to dusk during the holy month of *Ramadan*.

- *Zakat*: Muslims must pay two per cent income tax to be used for the poor.

- Pilgrimage: Muslims must perform the ritual pilgrimage (*Haj*) to Mecca at least once in their lifetime.

Understanding Islam and the law

The prevailing legal system in Saudi Arabia, known as the *Shari'a* is strictly based on the *Qur'an*. All people are considered equal before God. Everyone living in Saudi Arabia is subject to *Shari'a* law, non-Muslims as well as Muslims. While some punishments have received much publicity and seem harsh, the Saudis do claim to have a very low crime rate.

In general, expatriates living in Saudi Arabia must use common sense and be very aware of their conduct and dress in public. If they are caught breaking the laws publicly they will be punished in the same way as a Saudi national. This may involve long prison sentences and lashes, even the death penalty. The British Consular office makes it clear in a publication entitled *Living in Saudi Arabia, A Brief Guide*, that **'A British Consul cannot save UK nationals from the consequences of their own actions or negligence'**. (See Chapter 5, page 89.)

Points to remember
- Drinking, brewing and smuggling of alcoholic beverages is forbidden. Offenders caught smuggling or distributing alcohol will receive a prison sentence. Lashes and heavy fines may also be part of the penalty.

- Smuggling of drugs is a capital offence, and **the death penalty is enforced**. Possession of even small amounts can bring a prison sentence.

- Murder, adultery and homosexual acts can be punished by the death penalty. In some cases of accidental death the family of the victim may accept 'blood money'. Adultery cases require four male witnesses, hearsay is not accepted as evidence.

- The public practice of any religion but Islam is prohibited, and can result in a prison sentence, fines and deportation.

- Attempts to convert Muslims to another religion are prohibited.

- Non-Muslims are barred from entering mosques.

- Non-Muslims are prohibited from entering the holy cities of Mecca and Medina.

Shari'a legal system

There are four levels of courts under the *Shari'a* system. Each court deals with a different type of offence. There is an appeal process (see Chapter 5, page 91). The *Shari'a* legal system requires three judges to try a case. In both civil and criminal proceedings a *qadhi* acts as judge and jury. Civil claims may also be referred to the *Emir* (Governor) of a province. Commercial disputes may be arbitrated by chambers of commerce in key cities.

What the British Consul can do if you are arrested
- visit people in custody after notification of arrest
- provide a list of local lawyers
- give advice on local procedures
- liaise with local sponsors and authorities to provide doctors, if necessary
- notify next-of-kin if wished.

For more details see Chapter 5, page 94.

Islam and the social life of the Kingdom

The social and moral code of Islam influences every aspect of daily life in Saudi Arabia. Before dawn the *Azan* sounds from minarets of mosques on every block, calling the faithful to *Fajr*, the first obligatory prayer of the day. No longer does the *Muezzin* climb the minaret stairs; technology has brought the age of the loudspeaker, which can reach considerably further than the unaided human voice.

Clothing
Out on the streets Saudi men wear the traditional white *thobe*, with the red and white or plain white headcloth (*ghutrah*) secured by the *igaal*, the looped black head band which supposedly derives from ropes used to hobble camels in the desert.

Saudi women are completely covered under the immense black cloak known as an *abaya*. Their faces are veiled, either totally covered by black cloth or with just a slit for the eyes. Once a girl reaches puberty she must never show her face except among other women or men of her immediate family. Tradition has it that the custom arose during the centuries of tribal raiding. Despite the ferocity of the raids there were strict rules; animals and property could be seized, but not the wives as long as they kept their faces covered. There are also religious injunctions that women should cover themselves.

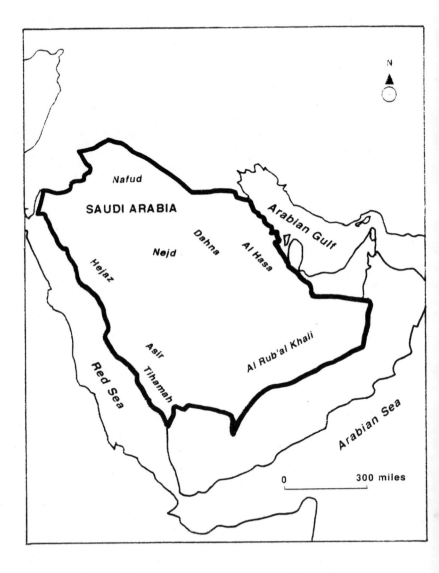

Fig. 2. Saudi Arabia: geographic regions.

Prayer time closing

As midday approaches the call to the second prayer, *Dhuhr*, is the signal that all shops must close. Closure of shops during prayer times is twenty to thirty minutes, depending on which prayer call it is. Customers are hustled out onto the streets, shutters screech and shops are locked. Staff wait outside until prayers are over to reopen. Prayer time closing is unique to Saudi Arabia. As the last two prayers of the day occur immediately before sunset (*Maghrib*) and an hour after sunset (*Isha*) it means early evening shopping sorties have to be carefully timed. Saudis themselves usually do their major shopping after the last prayer at night when it is cooler.

Restaurants too must observe prayer time closing and sometimes diners are hustled out mid-meal. In other cases, if the customers have already ordered they are locked in until prayers are over. Often it is impossible to call a taxi during prayer time. The local television stations also take an obligatory pause at prayer call.

Segregation of the sexes

Any form of intimacy between unmarried couples is discouraged in Islam. This segregation is ensured in many ways, which makes Saudi Arabia different even from other Gulf countries. There are no public cinemas in the Kingdom. Restaurants either prohibit women or have a men only section for men on their own and a family section where women and families may sit. A woman is not supposed to travel in a car with a man other than her husband, father, brother, or a professional driver. Hospitals have 'ladies' waiting rooms. Public buses have separate sections for women. There are special 'ladies' branches of banks.

Avoiding causing offence

- Men and women, even married couples, should not display affection in public, *ie* holding hands, arms round each other, even kissing goodbye at the airport.

- In Saudi Arabia it is common and socially acceptable for men to hold hands in public. Don't react negatively and don't pull your hand away if a Saudi business partner holds your hand for longer than you are accustomed to.

- Men should not automatically try to shake hands when introduced to an Arab woman, unless she indicates it is okay by making the first move.

- Women should not be overly friendly to Arab men in public. It may be misinterpreted as a 'come on'.

Ramadan

Ramadan is the ninth month of the year according to the *Hejira* calendar. All Muslims are required to abstain from food, drink and sexual intercourse from dawn to dusk. This is strictly observed in Saudi Arabia. While the Saudis appreciate that non-Muslims are not fasting, expatriates should refrain from eating, drinking, smoking or even chewing gum in public during *Ramadan*. If an expat is caught breaking the *Ramadan* fast he will be given a warning. A second infraction will result in a week's prison sentence.

At dusk a cannon usually signals the end of the fast each day. Traffic at this time can be particularly hectic. Traditionally *Ramadan* is the time for much visiting and entertaining, as families and friends get together to share the 'break fast' meal or *Iftar*. Shops usually re-open round 9 pm and stay open until midnight. A large meal is eaten just before dawn when the fast begins again.

The fasting, late nights and lack of sleep have a distinct effect on all aspects of life within the Kingdom. Business, postal services and visa procedures move much more slowly during this month. It is best to avoid any business trips to Saudi Arabia during *Ramadan*. Since the *Hejira* calender uses lunar months of twenty-nine or thirty days it is eleven days shorter than the year according to the Greogorian calendar.

Ramadan ends with the official sighting of the new moon beginning the next month.

Eid al Fitr

Muslims celebrate the end of *Ramadan* with the *Eid al Fitr* and there is a 3- or 4-day public holiday.

Haj

Haj is the prescribed ritual pilgrimage to Mecca which all Muslims should make at least once in their lifetime. *Haj* occurs two months after *Ramadan*. Over a million Muslims from all over the world travel to Mecca at this time, many of them flying into Jeddah. Saudi Arabia has a special Ministry of Haj, charged with the formidable task of housing, transporting and ensuring the health and safety of this massive influx of people. It is advisable, though, to avoid travelling to Jeddah for several weeks around this time.

Eid al Adha

Eid al Adha (Feast of the Sacrifice) immediately follows the pilgrimage of *Haj*. It is a time of sacrificial offerings and festivities which lasts four days. All businesses and government offices are closed during this holiday.

Food and drink

Muslims are prohibited from drinking intoxicating beverages. *The importation of any alcohol into the Kingdom is strictly forbidden.* Your luggage will be thoroughly checked upon arrival and there are severe penalties if you are caught. Even items such as wine yeast can bring heavy fines. Muslims are also forbidden to eat pork or any pork product. If you are caught trying to smuggle such products into the country they will be confiscated.

OBSERVING CUSTOMS AND COURTESIES

The more flexible and sensitive you are to Arab customs and culture, the more rewarding your experience will be in this unique country. Thousands of expatriates have spent years living and working here and enjoy it. Many have returned more than once. It is a vastly different culture, but the very differences are what make it so fascinating.

Making business contacts

As a business person, the more you are prepared to learn and appreciate different attitudes the more easily you will be able to adapt and develop new ways of solving problems.

This cultural assimilation is a two-way street. The Saudis have an ancient tradition of hospitality which has continued into the business world. Personal relationships are far more important in doing business in Saudi Arabia than many Western businessmen are accustomed to. Always remember that as a business visitor, or an expatriate living and working in the Kingdom, *your actions* will play a direct role in how the Saudis will judge your country and countrymen.

Some business dos and don'ts
- Do be patient. Be prepared to spend time getting to know your Saudi contacts before you discuss any business. Personal trust is vital. This may include numerous unscheduled visits for tea and

chats, or appointments where your Saudi contact breaks off for several lengthy phone calls.

- Don't be frustrated if your recommendations are not followed. The pace of change is slow and you may have to go over the same ground several times.

- Don't ever bring a gift before a deal is concluded, it may be considered as a bribe; bribes are prohibited and also highly offensive.

- Watch your language; Saudis are offended by swearing.

- Do not make social enquiries about a Saudi's wife or female members of his family.

- Avoid over-familiarity, such as using a Saudi's first name at initial meetings, unless requested to do so by the Saudi.

For more details see Chapter 4, page 70.

Making social contacts
As a family it is unlikely that you will have much contact with Saudi families. Saudi society is very family oriented and the trend towards expats living in compounds ensures the continued separation of local people from expatriates. Some expatriates, however, are fortunate enough to receive an invitation from their Saudi counterparts to attend a family function. If you live off-compound your wife may be invited by a Saudi neighbour to a ladies' party.

Some social dos and don'ts
- Saudi men and women usually entertain separately. Don't assume your wife is included in a dinner invitation.

- If you are invited to a small gathering reply to the invitation promptly and arrive at the appointed time.

- Show respect for any obviously older people by greeting them first.

- Saudis won't expect you to learn Arabic, but appreciate any attempts. The most common greeting is *As-salaam alaikum*, which means peace be upon you. The reply is *wa-alaikum as-salaam*, which means and upon you, peace.

- It is customary to drink up to three of the small Arabic style cups of cardamom-flavoured coffee, never more. Cover your cup with your hand or wiggle it to show you are finished.

- Do not attempt to bring up business discussions at a social gathering.

- Although before-dinner conversation is prolonged, guests are usually expected to leave shortly after the meal. An incense burner being passed around is often a signal that the party is over.

For more details see Chapter 4, page 70.

DISCUSSION POINTS

1. List five personal traits that will help make cultural assimilation to Saudi Arabia easier for you and your family.

2. Do you have the support of your family in your venture?

3. What are your goals in seeking to work and/or live in Saudi Arabia?

2

Getting There

VISA REQUIREMENTS STEP BY STEP

Saudi Arabia is one of the most difficult countries in the world to enter. There is no real tourist industry in the Kingdom and no casual visitors are allowed into the country. At check-in desks for Kingdom-bound flights you must show a valid current **entry visa** or you will not be allowed on the plane. The only people who will be granted visas to enter the country are:

- business visitors
- people with a contract to work for a Saudi sponsor company
- dependents of certain categories of people with contracts to work in the Kingdom
- immediate family relatives of people working in the Kingdom
- Muslims intending to perform their pilgrimage to Mecca
- nationals of other Gulf Cooperation Council (GCC) countries.

The procedure for obtaining a **visitor's business visa** to enter Saudi Arabia is complex and every step must be followed to the letter. The process can take from a few weeks to several months.

Business visas

In July 2000 the cost of a visit visa was 200 Saudi Riyals (SR). A visit visa may be issued for two weeks or three months. To avoid the loss of time and money in having a new visa issued, it is advisable to request the longest validity possible in case of unexpected delays. If you are planning several trips to the Kingdom, it is best to get a **multiple entry visa**. During your stay in the Kingdom you must carry your passport with you at all times.

Obtaining a visit visa for a business trip
To obtain a visit visa, you will need a Saudi sponsor to send a letter (or fax/telex) to the Saudi Embassy in London, or to an assigned

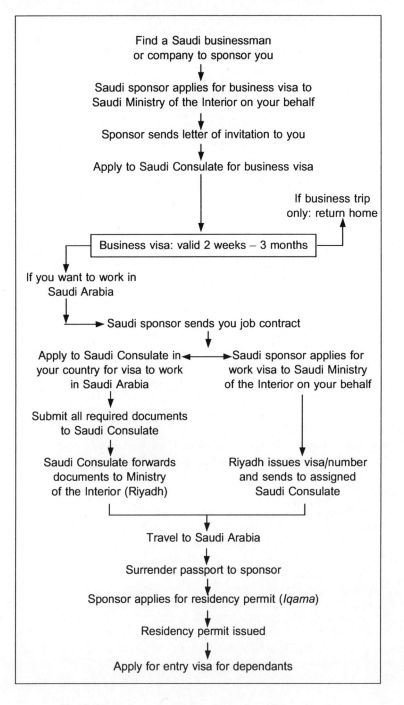

Fig. 3. How to get a working visa and residency permit.

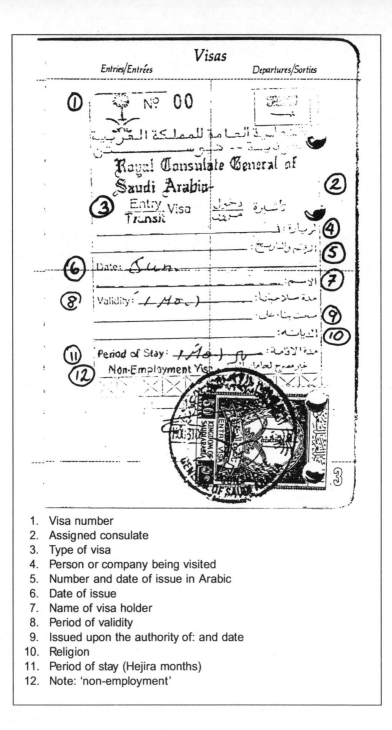

1. Visa number
2. Assigned consulate
3. Type of visa
4. Person or company being visited
5. Number and date of issue in Arabic
6. Date of issue
7. Name of visa holder
8. Period of validity
9. Issued upon the authority of: and date
10. Religion
11. Period of stay (Hejira months)
12. Note: 'non-employment'

Fig. 4. Saudi entry visa (business travel).

consulate if you happen to be outside the UK. This letter is a formal invitation from the Saudi sponsor, indicating he has applied on your behalf to the **Ministry of the Interior** for a visa to be issued to you and that authorisation will be sent to the assigned embassy. The invitation will include a visa number. When you know the visa number you can go to the embassy to collect your visa. Visas are issued by number and not by name. It is therefore essential to have the number or you will not be issued your visa.

The Royal Embassy of Saudi Arabia (including Consular Section) 30 Charles Street, London W1X 7PM. Tel: (020) 7917 3000.

Working visas
In order to work continuously in Saudi Arabia you must obtain **resident's status**. This process also starts with a visa. In this case you will need to prove you have a contract for a specific job, and can satisfy the required health, professional and education criteria.

You will need the following documents
- A copy of a signed contract offering a specified job with a Saudi sponsor company. Saudi sponsor companies usually have a 'block visa' from the Ministry of the Interior. The block visa has slots for specific job titles: *eg* one general manager, five construction supervisors, one secretary, two clerks and so on.

- A letter from the Saudi sponsor indicating he has applied to the Ministry of the Interior on behalf of the applicant, in order for him to receive a visa to fill a job slot.

- Education certificates.

- Medical certificates. This is a form obtainable from the Saudi Embassy/Consulate. The examination required is very detailed. An HIV test is required.

- A valid passport. Make sure your passport is valid for at least six more months. If you only have one or two empty pages left, it is best to get a new passport as Saudi visas will take up a whole page.

- Numerous passport-sized photos.

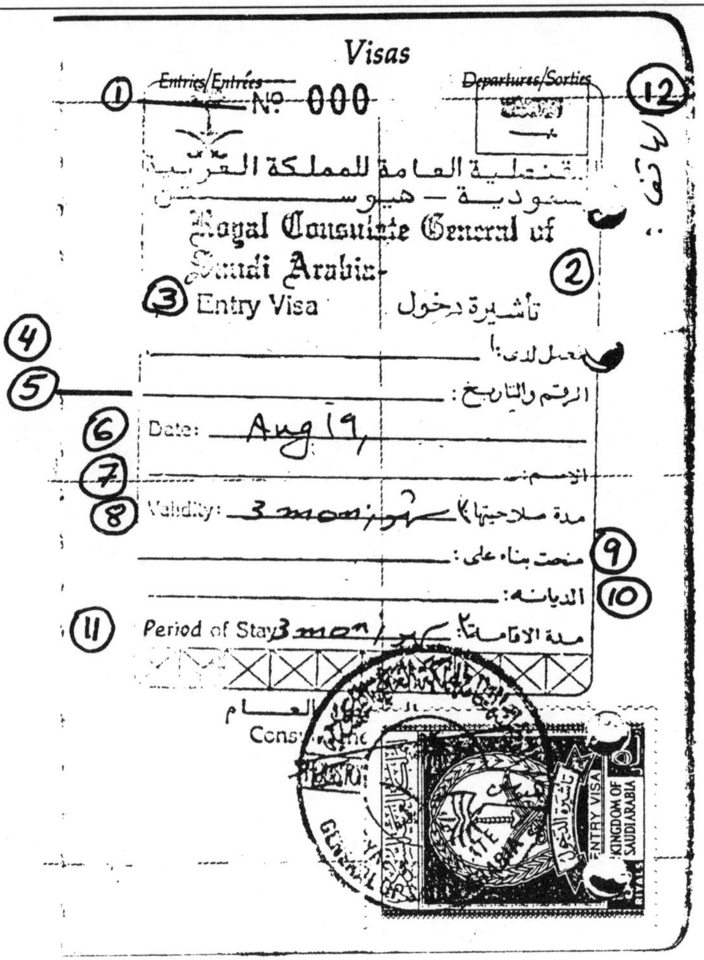

Fig. 5. Saudi entry visa (person with work contract and who will be applying for resident's status).

1. Visa number
2. Assigned consulate
3. Type of visa
4. Name of employer
5. Date and number of visa in Arabic
6. Date of issue
7. Name of visa holder
8. Period of validity (Hejira months)
9. Issued upon the authority of: and date
10. Religion
11. Period of stay
12. Contact telephone number

Once the Saudi authorities are satisfied with your qualifications, they will issue a **visa number** and send it by diplomatic pouch to the assigned embassy. Visas are filed by number not by name.

It is strongly recommended to use a **visa service** agent to assist you with your paperwork. This can save you the disappointment and expense of having to make several trips to London if your visa is not ready on the date given for pick-up. Visa Service Passports & Visas Worldwide, 2 Northdown Street, King's Cross, London N1. Tel: (020) 7833 2709. Fax: (020) 7833 1857.

ACQUIRING A RESIDENCE PERMIT

When you arrive in the Kingdom it is advisable to be met at the airport by your company's **Government Relations Representative** who must register you with the immigration authorities. He will apply for your *Iqama* (residence permit); the fee is SR 600 for one year or SR 2,000 for two years. He will then apply for your work permit. Companies usually pay these fees. Remember, you will need passport photos to accompany all the different forms.

Your entry visa serves as a temporary residence permit until you receive your *Iqama*. Once you receive your *Iqama* you must surrender your passport to your sponsor who will keep it while you are in the Kingdom. You must keep your *Iqama* with you at all times. When you leave Saudi Arabia on holiday you will need your sponsor to obtain an exit/re-entry visa for you. You will have to surrender your *Iqama* and your passport will be returned to you for your trip. You can only leave the country if there is an exit/re-entry visa stamped in it. If you are leaving the country and not returning, you will be issued an exit-only visa.

When you have your *Iqama* you can get a Saudi Driver's Licence. If you have a valid UK driver's licence, no driving test is required, only an eye and blood test. You must present your driver's licence and pay SR 500, plus a fee for translating your licence into Arabic. (SR 3 per line or SR 30 per page). Saudi Licences are valid for five years. Women are not permitted to drive in the Kingdom. International Driver's Licences are not valid in the Kingdom.

Note: the fees listed are current for 2000.

Entry for your dependants

Usually only managerial-level job holders are entitled to have their

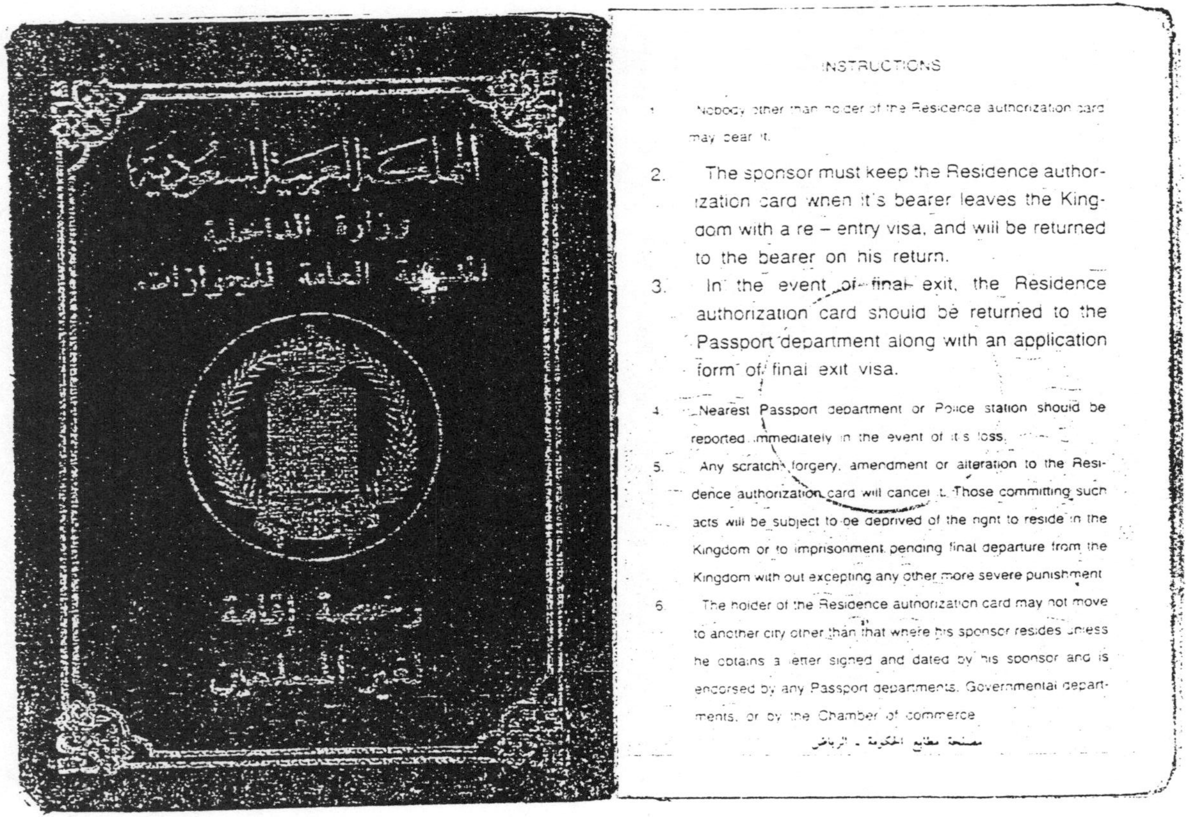

Fig. 6. Residence permit (*Iqama*).

wives and children reside with them in Saudi Arabia. The job holder must obtain his *Iqama* before he can apply for visas for his family. It can take several months before their visas are issued. If you plan to sell your house, or rent it while you are away, you should make arrangements for your family's accommodation in case there are unexpected delays in obtaining their visas.

You will need the following documents to obtain visas for your family
- original marriage certificates, certified by the Saudi Consulate in country of origin
- original birth certificates, certified by the Saudi Consulate in country of origin
- education certificates, certified by the Saudi Consulate in country of origin
- about a dozen passport-sized photos of each member of the family
- designated health certificates (forms obtainable from the Saudi Embassy/Consulate)
- passports with at least six months' validity before they expire (each child should have their own passport; see below).

Points to remember
Details in the procedure for obtaining a visa change all the time. Informal changes are made without published announcements. It is vital to check with the Saudi Consulate to get the latest information before making any assumptions. Above all, do not expect anything to happen quickly. Allow yourself plenty of time.

Arabic text will always take precedence over English text. Islamic (*Hejira*) calendar dates will always take precedence over Gregorian calendar dates and time limitations; *eg* if the information on a document is valid for two months, this means two lunar months, which is several days shorter than the Gregorian calendar months.

It is advisable to have a separate passport for each member of the family, even small children. If you have a child included on a parent's passport the authorities may refuse to allow you to travel out of Saudi Arabia without being accompanied by that child. (See Case Study below).

Check the date *Ramadan* begins and ends, as it will significantly slow the progress in obtaining your visa. The *Eid al Fitr* holiday at the end of *Ramadan* can add another ten days to two weeks in obtaining your visa.

Conversion table of Hejira to Gregorian calendar dates – tentative

Hejira Year	New Year	Ramadan begins	Eid al-Fitr	Eid al-Adha
1421	08.04.00	27.11.00	08.01.00 27.12.00	16.03.00
1422	28.03.01	16.11.01	16.12.01	05.03.01
1423	17.03.02	05.11.02	05.12.09	22.02.02

In 1997 the Saudi Government reversed its ruling that non-Muslim children could not attend school in the Kingdom after age 15. Since then many of the international schools catering to expatriates have expanded their services and now provide schooling up to age 17 or 18. Prior to the 1997 ruling non-Muslim children over 15 had to continue their education at boarding schools elsewhere.

Bringing your pet

It is best to check with the Saudi Consulate to find out the latest regulations regarding bringing pets into the Kingdom. At present it is relatively easy to bring cats. Your pet will need a rabies injection and a health certificate from your vet.

Dogs are more difficult to bring in since they are regarded as 'unclean' animals by Muslims. Officially only guard dogs and hunting dogs can be imported. It is possible that your vet may be able to substantiate your claim that your dog fulfils one of these criteria. Dogs require a rabies injection, and a health certificate which must be certified by the Saudi Consulate.

Both British Airways and KLM airlines provide good service for transporting animals to Saudi Arabia. On KLM flights animals are held in transit quarantine kennels in Amsterdam on the way.

Points to remember
- Your animal will be subject to six months' quarantine upon return to the UK.
- There are very few kennel facilities in Saudi Arabia.
- You may have to leave your animal with friends while you are on leave.

Some veterinary contacts with British veterinary staff
Jeddah Veterinary Clinic, Al Mutlaq Compound, Al Khobar. Tel: (03) 857 3079. Fax: (03) 859 1408.

Jeddah Veterinary Clinic, Prince Abdullah Bin Abdul Aziz St, Jeddah. Tel: (02) 691 4614/691 2896. Fax: (02) 691 4614.

P.A.W.S. (People's Animal Welfare Society)
P.A.W.S. is a volunteer organisation located in the Al Khobar area. They will find a dog-sitter for your pet while you are on home leave. When required they will refer you to a vet for your pet. They also find homes for abandoned pets.

BEFORE YOU LEAVE HOME

If you are planning to work in Saudi Arabia for more than a year, and especially if your family will be moving to the Kingdom, there are numerous personal and business affairs which you should take care of before you leave.

Arranging taxes
You should check with your local tax office to confirm your allotted tax status. Ask for a form P85 and submit it along with as much supporting documentation as possible, including a copy of your contract of employment. You may be eligible for a tax refund if you have paid tax calculated on a full year's earnings. Also, by confirming your new tax status, you will avoid problems which may occur when you return to the UK.

Sorting out property
You may decide to sell your house before you leave. Alternatively, it can make sense to rent your house while you are away; the house is not left empty, a prey to thieves and weather damage. You are also covering mortgage and insurance costs.

On the other hand, many expats leave the Kingdom for an extended period during the hot Arabian summer. If you and/or your family plan to return to the UK you may prefer to stay in your own home rather than impose on friends or relatives. Families with older children at boarding school in the UK may prefer to come home during the school holidays rather than bring the children to the Kingdom. It is a matter of personal choice.

Checklist of other personal arrangements

- update your will
- insure any household goods in storage
- arrange with your bank for transferring of funds
- arrange for the payment of bills in the UK
- make sure you have adequate insurance coverage
- arrange to have mail forwarded.

TO TAKE OR NOT TO TAKE

Assuring personal health

If you, or a member of your family, suffer from any chronic condition or allergies, seek advice from your GP on how the hot climate may affect you. Get extra supplies of prescription medicines. If your medicine contains alcohol, you may need to find a substitute. Also check with the Saudi Embassy/Consular section for the latest immunisation (injections) requirements. For further information on health issues see Chapter 7, page 124.

Choosing which clothes to take

- Plenty of clothes in natural fabrics, *eg* cotton, linen, silk.

- The emphasis is on comfortable, casual wear. In Riyadh men wear suits to work, but in the Eastern Province they are more informal. Since women have to be careful about what they wear in public, they tend to dress more casually than fashionably.

- Mid-calf or long skirts; long, loose tops for wearing in public. Shorts and tee-shirts are fine on the compound.

- Bring a few jerseys and at least one jacket; nights and early mornings can be very cold.

- Plenty of swimwear. They wear out quickly due to the hot sun and chlorine.

- Women may prefer to bring plenty of 'intimate garments' as the styles available in the Kingdom may not be to their taste. (See Chapter 7, page 115).

- Dark sunglasses, or preferably a range of shades for different conditions. All sunglasses should have UVA and UVB protection.

Taking household goods

In most cases you will be provided with housing, or a housing allowance, which will enable you to rent furnished accommodation. It will therefore not be necessary to bring a house-load of furniture with you to Saudi Arabia.

While you will want to make your new house as comfortable and homelike as possible, it is wise not to send anything you would not be able to replace if it were damaged or lost in transit. Normally an employer will pay for a specified amount of personal goods to be shipped, and in some cases a small air freight allowance may be included in the contract. Check what your weight allowance will be.

What not to take

All shipments of goods arriving in Saudi Arabia are thoroughly examined by customs inspectors, who will confiscate prohibited items and fine you. The following items are prohibited in Saudi Arabia:

- firearms and ammunition
- alcohol or alcoholic beverages or anything pertaining to their manufacture
- narcotics, unless accompanied by a doctor's prescription
- pork or any pork products (including that in medicines, *eg* insulin)
- books or magazines depicting nudity (bathing suits, lingerie catalogues and art books included)
- pornographic material of any type
- hand-held transmitters (including children's toy walkie-talkies)
- Christmas trees and decorations
- non-Muslim religious material of any type
- statues of the human form.

It is a good idea to check through everything you intend to send, even family beach photographs. All books, computer disks, CDs, audio and video tapes will be retained by the Ministry of Information, which is looking for pornography, nudity, religious material and politically controversial material. Anything considered unsuitable will be confiscated and you may be fined or, in extreme cases, jailed or even deported.

SENDING YOUR GOODS

Make a detailed inventory and valuation of all the items you plan to ship. This will be needed for insurance and customs purposes. Find out what your moving allowance is, weight-wise and/or cost-wise. Your company may require you to get estimates from several removal firms. It is best to arrange door-to-door service. This will cost more, but it will save you headaches at the other end, particularly if you will be living a long way from the port of entry. If you arrange for door-to-port you will be responsible for arranging customs clearance and transporting your household goods to your home.

Time frame for shipments and customs clearance

• Air shipments take three to seven days. If shipped by Saudia Airlines or British Airways, the shipment is sent directly to Saudi Arabia and arrives within a couple of days. More time is required if shipping by Egypt Air due to a stopover in Cairo.

• Allow thirty-five days for sea freight to Jeddah or Dammam.

• Customs clearance for air freight takes two to four days; sea freight takes four to seven days.

• If your shipment arrives during *Ramadan*, or during one of the two major holidays, customs clearance will take longer.

Air shipments
Air freight is very expensive, but can be preferable for small shipments of up to 400 lbs. Here is a list of some items you might prefer to send by air:

• essential kitchen equipment
• extra clothes
• some towels and bedlinen
• children's toys and games
• hobby items.

Do not send computer disks, video tapes or books by air freight. They will be retained by the Ministry of Information, who will view them for any material which is considered offensive. It can take months to get them back.

Surface shipments
Can be used for:

- framed pictures and ornaments
- crockery and cutlery
- computer, printer and software
- bedlinen and towels
- sports equipment
- children's toys and games
- books
- audio and video tapes (see note on video tapes above)
- hobby materials and tools
- sewing machine
- extra glasses, and eye prescription or extra contact lens cleaning materials
- extra supplies of any prescription medicines and copies of prescriptions.

Working out extra costs

Demurrage
Demurrage costs (*ie* storage if your shipment arrives more than ten days before you), customs duty (20 per cent furniture, 12 per cent other items, books are exempt), port dues and inspection costs are all charged on top of the door-to-door cost. Find out if your company will pay these costs.

Removal companies
The following removal companies in Saudi Arabia frequently work with expatriates:

Four Winds, PO Box 5921, Dammam 31432, Saudi Arabia. Tel: (03) 857 4434. Fax: (033) 857 4841.

Other offices: Jeddah (head office). Tel: (02) 691 8883; Riyadh. Tel: (01) 454 4080; Jubail. Tel: (03) 361 3202; Al Khobar. Tel: (03) 864 9671; Tabuk. Tel: (04) 421 0467; Yanbu. Tel: (04) 322 8429.

Namma Cargo, PO Box 1498, Al Khobar 31952. Tel: (03) 895 2222.

Other offices: Jeddah. Tel: (02) 672 1251/2645, Fax: (02) 671 3410; Jubail. Tel: (03) 341 7173/7178, Fax: (03) 341 7042; Riyadh. Tel: (01) 463 1163/465 4200, Fax: (01) 465 7641; Yanbu. Tel: (04) 321 0829,

Fax: (04) 396 2250.

The following companies in the UK specialise in international removals:

Scotpac International (UK) Ltd, Security House, Abbey Wharf Ind Estate, Kingsbridge Road, Barking, London IG11 0BT. Tel: (020) 8591 3388. Fax: (020) 8594 4571.

Scotpac International (UK) Ltd, Containerbase, Gartsherrie Road, Coatbridge ML5 2EL. Tel: (01236) 449666. Fax: (01236) 449888.

Allied Pickfords, 3–9 Willow Lane, Mitcham, Surrey CR4 4NA. Tel: 0800 289 229. Fax: (020) 8646 1973.

Arranging delivery of your shipment
Make sure you know who the local agent and carrier in Saudi Arabia will be. When you arrive, contact the local agent and give him your name, address and shipping information. You should have copies of:

- original airway bill or ocean bill of lading
- original inventory or packing list
- insurance certificate
- document transmittal.

Departing and arriving
When you fly, it is a good idea to have extra copies of your Saudi visa in a separate place from your passport. Many flights into Saudi Arabia arrive at night. There are often long queues to get through the immigration checkpoint. If it is your first time in the Kingdom, it will take longer to check your passport and visa details. Be patient.

Residence visas are now computer readable so the time spent in the immigration process has been greatly reduced. Businessmen who have to make repeated trips to Saudi Arabia can now obtain multiple entry visas which are good for two years.

Once past passport control you may be approached by porters in the arrivals hall who will say they can get you through customs easily, for a charge. Be warned. In the past everyone had their luggage opened and checked. Recently customs personnel have started to use X-ray machines to check baggage instead of routinely opening every item. Anecdotal evidence indicates that women travelling on their own, or with small children, sometimes get through with only a brief check. Men travelling on their own usually have the contents of their luggage minutely examined. Unsuitable books, magazines, religious material, pork and alcohol are immediately confiscated if found, and you may be fined.

CASE STUDIES

An English couple's trip to Bahrain is cancelled

An English couple had been living in Al Khobar for six months. They were fortunate enough to have multiple exit/re-entry visas, which had enabled them to make two weekend trips across the Causeway to nearby Bahrain during that time. Each time they had taken their 4-year old son with them.

They planned to celebrate the wife's birthday by driving across the Causeway and spending the evening having dinner in Bahrain. This time they did not take their son with them. At the Saudi passport checkpoint on the Causeway, the official stopped the wife. He asked why her son was not travelling with her since he was included on her passport. She explained they were only going for the evening and had left the boy with a babysitter. The official apologised, but said that since her son was on her passport she was not allowed to travel out of the country without being accompanied by him. The couple had to retrace their steps and eat dinner in Al Khobar.

A businessman pays for confusing dates

A businessman had to make a business trip to Dubai. He obtained an exit/re-entry visa which was valid for two months. The date the visa was issued was stamped in his passport. His business trip was re-scheduled several times.

When at last he could make his trip there were only two days left before the two months expired. He was turned away by Saudi airport passport control because, according to the *Hejira* calendar, the two months had already expired, even though according to the Gregorian calender he had two days left. He had to pay a fine for allowing his visa to expire without being used, and pay for a new exit/re-entry visa.

3

Finding Accommodation

LIVING ON A COMPOUND

What is a compound and why choose to live there?

Saudi Arabia is virtually the only country in the Middle East where most Western expatriates live on compounds which isolate them from the Saudi community at large.

What is a compound? It is perhaps best described as a small, enclosed community where Europeans/Americans can feel at ease living amongst people from similar cultures who share the same customs and lifestyle. It has evolved as the customary housing situation for Western expatriates because the locals prefer not to have foreign cultures and influences spread amongst them. Behind the compound walls expatriates can also enjoy freedom to dress and socialise as they are accustomed, which is not possible in ordinary residential situations. Women, particularly, find a sense of personal safety and security on the compound, knowing that their children have more freedom to play outdoors because there is minimal traffic and the entrances have security guards.

Price range of compounds

Compound housing appears vastly expensive when compared to housing costs at home. Even more so since costs are usually quoted on a yearly, rather than a monthly, rate. Prices range from SR 40,000 p.a. up to SR 500,000 p.a. However, these prices usually include:

- furnishings
- utilities
- maintenance
- a range of services and facilities.

The old adage 'location, location, location' also holds for Saudi Arabia. Accommodation in the capital Riyadh is much more expensive than, for example, in Yanbu, (SR 146,000 plus SR 24,000 maintenance charge for a three-bedroom villa in Riyadh versus SR 115,000 inclusive of maintenance for a four-bedroom villa in Yanbu).

Lower-priced compounds
Compounds in the range SR 40,000 – SR 70,000 p.a. usually offer a basic range of facilities, such as:

- air conditioning
- telephone line
- swimming pool
- recreational centre
- tennis court
- children's playground
- school bus service
- shopping bus at least once daily.

Houses may be more like 'prefabs' or large mobile homes. The perimeter of the compound may be enclosed by a fence rather than a wall.

Mid-range compounds
For SR 80,000 – SR 85,000 p.a. one would expect a well maintained compound offering:

- air conditioned villas (regular houses are always called villas in the Kingdom)
- a swimming pool
- one or two tennis courts
- a recreation room where activities can be held
- a shopping/school bus service
- electricity
- water
- telephone (billed separately)
- carpets
- curtains
- washer
- dryer
- dishwasher
- fridge.

Many compounds in this range also have satellite dishes enabling residents to receive BBC World News, CNN and channels broadcasting movies, TV programmes and major sporting events. Some compounds now even offer Internet access.

Finding a villa to rent
Employers are required by law to provide employees with accommodation. Estate agents generally keep companies appraised of the housing market and housing availability. For those who are direct hires (see Chapter 5, page 88) your employer may give you a price range for your housing. You can go directly to an estate agent for assistance.

Using local newspapers
Another source for locating housing is the local newspaper. The *Arab News, Saudi Gazette* and the *Riyadh Daily* are English language newspapers which are distributed throughout the Kingdom and have daily advertisements for villas located on compounds and outside compounds within the cities.

Addresses of English language newspapers in the Kingdom:

Arab News, PO Box 4556, Jeddah 21433. Tel: (02) 639 1888/639 3223. Riyadh. Tel: (01) 441 9933.

Riyadh Daily, PO Box 851, Riyadh 11421. Tel: (01) 487 1000.

Saudi Gazette, PO Box 5576, Jeddah 21432. Tel: (02) 667 4020/667 4408. Riyadh. Tel: (01) 465 3324.

Finding accommodation through your company
Companies have two choices in housing their employees:

1. The company provides a list of compounds to the employee which he can then choose from.
2. The company houses their employees in one compound.

In Riyadh and the Dhahran area many new compounds have been built in the past four years and older compounds have been extensively refurbished. The Yanbu housing areas have grown tremendously in the last few years. Jubail is in the process of building compounds in order to accommodate their housing needs. There has not been the same building expansion in Jeddah.

Paying the rent

Companies typically set structured budgets according to an employee's job position. If his company has not already arranged housing for him, they may indicate the price level of his housing allowance and give him a list of compounds to look at. Although the employee makes the actual choice, the company will then sign the lease and pay twelve months' rent, plus damage deposit (around SR 5,000 – SR 10,000).

The housing market is highly competitive, consequently prices are often negotiable. In the past compound owners have preferred to be paid a year's rent in advance; the present competitive situation is making it possible for companies to negotiate half-yearly, or even quarterly, payments. The customer's position is stronger if he wants several villas at once. Sometimes a customer may be able to negotiate a price reduction in the form of thirteen months' rent for the price of a twelve-month lease.

What does furnished mean?

Most houses are fully furnished. This means carpets, curtains, furniture, appliances (washer, dryer, cooker, fridge and dishwasher), but not cooking utensils, crockery, bedlinen and towels. Occasionally it is possible for a company, or employee, to negotiate a 'soft pack' which includes cooking utensils, crockery, bedlinen and towels. The soft pack is usually provided in the form of a money allowance which either a company representative, or the employee, then uses to purchase the items. A soft pack for a three-bedroomed villa, which is considered to be a maximum six-person occupancy, will typically include kitchen utensils, crockery and cutlery for six, plus towels and a change of bedlinen for each bedroom.

What kind of appliances should I bring?

Compound villas are usually wired for American appliances with 110v or 120v (but there are 220v/240v outlets for heavy duty appliances, such as washing machines). It is possible to have the compound maintenance servicemen rewire individual outlets for 220v or 240v usage, but do not expect to bring numerous European household appliances and be able to plug them in without some problems. It is also advisable to buy a television locally, as British or American television sets often don't work properly in the Kingdom. There is a good range of multi-system televisions available locally which can use American (NTSC) or British (PAL) videos, and prices are reasonable.

CHOOSING A COMPOUND

- Ask around for personal recommendations. Colleagues who have been living in the Kingdom may know about the advantages or disadvantages of compounds within the permitted price range.

- Visit the compound and have a good look around. Does it appear well kept? Are the lawns and flower beds well tended? Is there rubbish lying around? These are good indicators of the management style and whether maintenance requests on your villa will be carried out promptly.

- Check out the gate guard on duty. Does he appear alert and conscientious? A sloppy appearance can be a clue to sloppy management style.

- Ask about the bus services. Does the school bus go to the school your children will be attending? How frequently are the shopping bus services scheduled? This will affect a wife's morale and to what extent she will have to depend on her husband to carry out essential errands.

- Ask about the tap water. Most compounds have water treatment facilities and the water is referred to as 'sweet', *ie* not saline-tasting, and can be used for cooking and drinking. You may prefer to buy bottled water for drinking and cooking. Ask about water delivery companies, *eg* Aqua Cool.

- Central air conditioning can be preferable to individual room units, because it is less noisy. However, it can be more expensive to run if you are paying your own utilities.

- Think about the size of the compound and how this fits in with your own lifestyle. Some compounds are clusters of tightly packed concrete villas with little private space. Older compounds often have more shade trees and green space.

- Ask about the 'demographic' make-up of the compound. If you have children who yearn for playmates, it will be preferable to live amongst families with children. Conversely, if you have no children, or they are grown, you may prefer the quiet of other childless couples.

WHAT YOU SHOULD BEWARE OF IN A LEASE AGREEMENT

- Company representatives and individuals should read the fine print of rental agreements carefully. There may be odd restrictions like no car washing on the compound, no pets, and so on.

- If you have negotiated a price discount, for example thirteen months for the price of a twelve-month lease, be aware that this price is good only for the period of the lease. After thirteen months the lease may go back up to the original price.

- When negotiating, companies should consider covering themselves for the eventuality of having contracts cancelled, or if other situations arise which require moving employees out of the Kingdom. It is very difficult to get out of a lease. However, you can usually give thirty days' notice if you are not renewing the lease. A thirty-day notification is also applicable on a six-month lease.

FINDING ACCOMMODATION OFF-COMPOUND

Some companies give their employees a housing allowance. The employee is then responsible for finding his own accommodation. It is perfectly possible to rent a villa, or apartment, privately rather than live on a compound. The three English language dailies, the *Arab News*, *Saudi Gazette* and *Riyadh Daily*, all have advertisements for accommodation in the major cities. There are also several estate agents who will help you find accommodation to suit your price range.

Choosing an estate agent
The easiest way to choose an estate agent is to have a good look at the area of the city you will be working in, and select housing within that area which appeals to you. Then contact the estate agents for that area. Even though the estate agent may speak fluent English, it is advisable to take an Arabic speaker with you, especially when it comes to the fine points of a leasing agreement.

Points to remember
- Rent is normally paid a year in advance.

- Estate agents charge five per cent commission, half paid by the tenant and half by the owner.

- All routine maintenance is the responsibility of the tenant.

- If you spend your own money on improvements, the rent may be increased.

Introducing the Arab-style home

Private homes in Saudi Arabia tend to be very large, with little garden space and high walls round them. To facilitate the strict segregation of men and women required by Saudi custom, there are separate entrances and sections of the house for men and women. The front entrance, sitting room and bathroom is for the men. Women usually enter by a side door, and have their own sitting room and bathroom near the kitchen at the back of the house. There are a lot of doors everywhere and frequently a lot of wasted space. Bathrooms often have a bidet or a hose-like device beside the toilet for washing oneself after using the toilet.

What do I get for my money?

Standards of accommodation on the private market vary enormously. Some villas/apartments have telephone line, carpets, furniture, air conditioning and fitted kitchens. At the other end of the spectrum some accommodation may only have a tap in the kitchen, with no sink or cabinets, no carpets, no air conditioning (only holes in the wall for the units) and hole-in-the-floor style toilets.

Prices for private villas range from around SR 40,000 at the bottom end, to SR 120,000 at the upper end of the market, though obviously there are more luxurious villas available at much higher prices. Apartments range from as low as SR 6,000 for a very basic one-bedroom bachelor's apartment, to two- and three-bedroom models at SR 30,000. Some newer apartment buildings, which offer fully carpeted and furnished apartments, are SR 40,000 – SR 50,000. This is for a full year's rent. It is sometimes possible to negotiate payment on a six-month basis. Prices are slightly higher in the Dhahran-Khobar-Dammam area than in Riyadh.

If you have to furnish a home, secondhand furniture tends to be expensive in the Kingdom (see Chapter 7, page 113). The advantage is that it will retain its value, so items such as air conditioning units, furniture, appliances, even cars, have a high resale value on the local market.

Checking your lease

● The lease should clearly state the beginning and end dates.

● Unless clearly stated otherwise, all leases are based on the Islamic (*Hejira*) calendar (see Chapter 5, page 90), so the lease will be eleven days shorter per year.

● If there are any problems with the house (chipped tiles, ceiling lights without a fixture, peeling wallpaper, *etc*), have them clearly stated in the lease to avoid accusations when you leave.

● If you have to buy equipment, such as kitchen cabinets, air conditioners, make sure you include a list of the items purchased and a clause which states you will take them with you when you leave, otherwise the landlord may try to claim them.

● The lease should state the minimum notice the tenant/owner is required to give to vacate the property.

● Check that all phone and utilities bills have been paid.

● Include a clause which states that you are not responsible for any liens or payments against the property.

Telephone and utilities

Telephones
If your villa or apartment does not already have a phone line, it may take many months, or even years, to get one, depending on how much demand there is for lines in that particular area. To obtain a telephone line you can apply at the Saudi Telephone Office and your name will be put on a waiting list. This will cost a few hundred riyals.

There are unorthodox routes of obtaining telephone lines, which can operate much quicker, but can cost **several thousand riyals**. When you move on you can then sell the telephone line.

Water and electricity
You will be billed monthly for electricity; annually for water. All bills are written in Arabic and the *Hejira* calendar applies. Public water supplies throughout the Kingdom are officially suitable for cooking and drinking purposes. In practice, however, the water tends to be very alkaline in some areas, which affects the taste, and

also makes it hard on kettles and washing clothes. The pipes in a particular building may also affect the quality of water. Many people prefer to buy bottled water, or have it delivered in 19-litre bottles by services such as Aqua Cool (coupons for 25 bottles typically cost SR 220). There are also fill-up points in some areas where you can take your own large container and fill it free of charge. You will use considerably more water in the summer months.

Terminating your lease

If you intend to move at the end of your twelve-month lease it is customary to give one or two months' notice. Make your intentions clear well in advance. If you do not give notice, and continue to stay in a property after the expiration of your twelve-month lease, you may be automatically charged another full year's rent. On the other hand, if the landlord decides he wants the property before the lease has expired you may have to move with less than a month's notice.

Generally, estate agents do not ask for a damage deposit on private villa leases, but you are expected to leave the property in good condition. This can be tricky in cases where after a few days of living in a property you discover power points not working, or other hidden problems. The owner may demand his property returned in better condition than when you moved in.

Living off-compound

Some advantages
- much cheaper than living on a compound
- privacy for families
- not subjected to compound gossip
- not living with the people you work with
- children not squabbling on the school bus.

Some disadvantages
- responsible for all maintenance
- women have to depend on taxis or lifts for transport, unless you can afford a driver
- have to plan social visits for the children and provide transport to activities
- children cannot ride their bicycles out in the streets
- Arabic neighbours may keep different hours; noise at nights.

SINGLE STATUS ACCOMMODATION

Many people who work in Saudi Arabia are on a **single status contract**. Housing is usually provided by the employer. People working on a single status contract will be assigned to 'men's' or 'women's' accommodation, with strict regulations on visitors and, in the case of women, a curfew.

Resources to help in your housing search

There are now a number of Internet websites which provide information on compounds, housing and living conditions in Saudi Arabia. Go to *www.arab.net* and explore the **Arabian Homes** sites and **Mura Bustan Compound** sites. These give information (albeit somewhat glamourised for advertising purposes) about compounds, with details about shopping, bus services, recreational facilities and pictures of homes. They can be contacted directly as follows:

Arabian Homes, Tel: 966 2 682 2201 x752. Fax: 966 2 683 4560.
    Email: *sales@arabian-homes.com.sa*
Mura Bustan. Tel: 966 2 691 0041. Fax: 966 2 682 6646. Email:
    info@mura-bustan.com.sa

BRIEF CITY PROFILES

Jeddah

Jeddah, located on the Red Sea, is a city of nearly 2 million people. It is Saudi Arabia's largest port and, for centuries, has been a landing point for pilgrims from all over the Muslim world on their way to Mecca. Until the early 1980s it was still largely the business and diplomatic centre of Saudi Arabia. The centre of Jeddah still retains some well preserved historic buildings, but the city has largely been modernised, especially the glamorous Corniche coastline. The climate is hot and humid and the traffic hectic.

Supermarkets
Sarawat (selection more British), Safeway (selection more American).

Clothes
BHS and Mothercare for children.

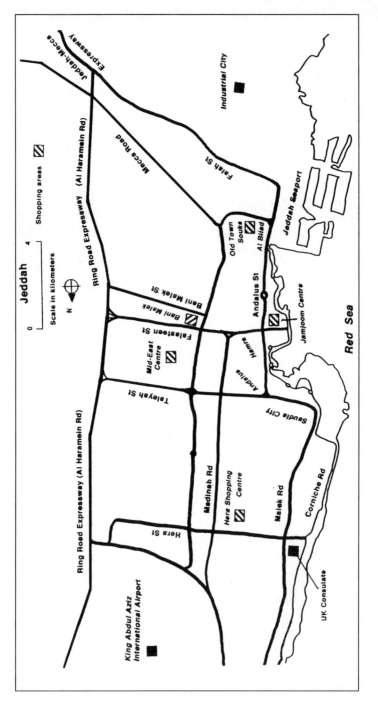

Fig. 7. Map of Jeddah.

Shopping centres
Jamjoom Shopping Centre, International Market (oldest but most popular), Camel Centre downtown next to old *Suq* (see Chapter 7, page 108).

Toys
Very good selection (see Chapter 7, page 119).

Hobby supplies
Good selection (see Chapter 7, page 116).

Antiques
Good selection (see Chapter 7, page 119).

Restaurants
The Red Sea Palace Hotel (642 8555), the Marriott (671 4000) and Regency (652 1234) are recommended for Friday brunch, Intercontinental (661 1800). There are numerous cafés in the old town area and many fast food restaurants in the city.

Car hire
Avis (661 0925), Budget (669 3384), Hertz (660 5301 and 661 0653).

Hospitals
GNP (Dr Ghassan N. Pharaon) Hospital offers medical and dental care. Tel: 682 0289. The GNP also has a Well Woman Programme. Tel: 682 3200 ext 264. (GNP has branches in Riyadh, Yanbu, Abha, Jizan, Najran, Buraidah, Taif, Al Baha and Tabuk.) For more extensive information see Chapter 8, 'Health care'.

Schools
The Continental School (member of Saudi Arabian International Schools – British Section) accredited by European Council of International Schools, PO Box 6453, Jeddah 21442. Tel: 699 3936. Fax: 699 1943. The Continental School has now added classes for students over 15 years old. Jeddah Preparatory School (SAIS British-Dutch Section), PO Box 6316, Jeddah 21442. Tel: 654 2354. Fax: 238 0232.

Organisations
British Women's Group Jeddah, c/o British Consulate General, PO Box 393, Jeddah 21411. Tel: 654 1811. Commercial section hours: 8.00 am to 3.00 pm; Consular section hours: 8.30 am to 12.00 noon.

Activities
Excellent location for snorkelling and diving in the Red Sea. Sailing and windsurfing are also popular. Windsurfing boards must be registered as sailboats. You can buy membership to private beaches, *eg* at some of the hotels where it is possible to wear bathing suits and, on some, it is possible to rent air conditioned chalets.

Travel
Avoid making any air travel plans around the main *Haj* (pilgrimage) time as hundreds of thousands of pilgrims are arriving. The influx of people often brings diseases such as meningitis and you are advised to get preventative inoculations. Traffic also tends to be appalling at this time. Another area to explore from Jeddah is the cool mountainous region around Taif, a summer resort for many of the Saudi Royal family.

Yanbu
Yanbu actually consists of three distinct areas: Yanbu Al Bar on the Corniche, Yanbu Al Nakal located in the mountains, and Yanbu Al Sinaiyah which is inland. Yanbu is approximately 200 miles from Jeddah. There are three flights a day, five days a week, to Jeddah. The cost is approximately SR 200 economy, SR 510 first class per round trip (2000 prices). Because women are not allowed to drive in the Kingdom, arrangements must be made for transport in Jeddah. Flight reservations and transport arrangements are made through a travel agency.

The Yanbu area is a rapidly growing one and housing construction is underway to meet the demand. Unlike many areas in Saudi Arabia, Yanbu and her sister city Jubail have integrated neighbourhoods, not compound living. These neighbourhoods are referred to as 'camps' in many cases.

Within the Yanbu area there is a museum, zoo and park. Campers enjoy the desert area. The original village of Yanbu is Yanbu Al Bar, located on the Corniche. The home of Lawrence of Arabia is located in this area and is open to the public. Unfortunately, it now in ruins, but still of interest to history buffs.

The climate of the Yanbu area is hot and dry during the summer; the rest of the year is pleasant, resembling a Mediterranean spring.

Supermarkets
Supermarkets in Yanbu are called commissaries. There are eight to ten commissaries, located throughout the various camps. There are

four or five large commissaries.

Clothing
Shopping for clothing is rather limited, although more stores are opening. Generally, clothing is purchased in Jeddah or on home leave.

Antiques
Yanbu has a good selection of antiques, brass, copper, carpets and gold.

Toys
There are several toy stores.

Hobby supplies
Limited. Buy in Jeddah, or on home leave.

Restaurants
Holiday Inn, and the old Hyatt Hotel (now has a new name, but everyone still calls it the Hyatt). Many fast food, local, Chinese, Turkish.

Hospital
A full service hospital and clinic; has a good reputation.

School
International School. Tel: (04) 392 1088/9. Fax: (04) 392 1075.

Organisations
Yanbu Women's Group.

Activities
Tennis, camping, water sports, bridge, arts and crafts groups.

Travel
Airport located in Jeddah for international flights.

Riyadh
Riyadh, the capital of the Kingdom of Saudi Arabia, is a city of 2.5 million people located in the Central Province. The area around the city, known as the Najd region, is the heartland of the Al Saud clan. Many of the dress codes and other social restrictions are more

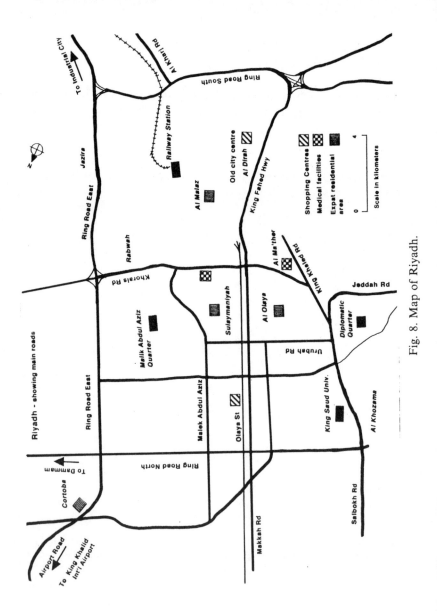

Fig. 8. Map of Riyadh.

60

strictly enforced here. All the foreign embassies are now located in Riyadh's purpose built diplomatic quarter. The largest concentrations of Western expats are in Malaz, Sulaimaniyah and Olaya districts. The climate is very hot and dry, with summer temperatures over 40°C, but winter nights can be very cold with temperatures as low as 8°C.

Supermarkets
Al Azizia, Euromarche, Al Sarawat, Tamimi Safeway.

Children's clothes
Mothercare, Olaya and Sitteen St. Al Akaria Centre, Osh Kosh B'Gosh (American), Olaya Al Akaria Centre; Jacardi (French), Sitteen St Al Akaria Centre.

Adults' clothes
Main shopping centres: Olaya Al Akaria, Shola, Al Najoud, Al Moussa, Sitteen Street (see Chapter 7, page 115).

Toys
Extensive selection, (see Chapter 7, page 119).

Hobby supplies
Very good (see Chapter 7, page 116).

Antiques
Very good selection (see Chapter 7, page 119).

Restaurants
French Corner (Debab St. and also diplomatic quarter) (488 0780); Intercontinental Hotel, The Oasis/Verandah (465 5000); Al Khozama Hotel, The Windrose (465 4650); Riyadh Marriotts, Al Ferdaus Steakhouse (477 9300); Bankok Seafood, across street from Olaya Al Akaria (465 1416).

Car hire
Budget (464 7116).

Hospitals
Al Hamadi (462 2000); Mishari (maternity specialist hospital) (465 7700); GNP Polyclinic (476 7597/98); Consulting Clinics (465 9100). (For more details, see Chapter 8, 'Health care'.)

Schools
British School Riyadh, PO Box 85769, Riyadh 11612 (248 2387).
The American School (491 4290) and the Multinational School (453
1686) have added classes for non-Muslim children over 15 years old.

Organisations
Women's Corona Group, PO Box 3843, Riyadh 11481; also contact
Riyadh British Embassy, PO Box 94351, Riyadh 11693. Tel: 488
0077/0088. Commercial section: 8.00 am to 3.00 pm. Consular
section: 8.30 am to 1.30 pm, Saturday to Wednesday.

Activities
Riyadh has many historical sites such as the Mismak Palace where
Abdul Aziz stormed the city in 1902; the Qasr al Murraba; the old
village of Dir'iyah. Camping trips within a few hours drive of the
city are also very popular. (See Chapter 8, 'Travelling in the
Kingdom'). A new national musuem is now open and well worth a
visit. The museum's telephone number is: 403 9961 or 402 950 ext.
1082.

Travel
Riyadh has an international airport served by major airlines: British
Airways. Tel: 465 7004; Air France. Tel: 476 9666; Emirates Airlines.
Tel: 465 7117; KLM. Tel: 477 4777; Lufthansa. Tel: 463 2004.

Dhahran/Dammam/Khobar
Previously this was referred to as Dhahran because that was the
name of the airport. The King Fahd International Airport opened in
November 1999 and the airport destination is now called Dammam.
Strictly speaking there is no town of Dhahran. This is only the name
of the former airport, and the ARAMCO work and residential
camp. A few kilometres away, Dammam is the main Saudi port on
the Arabian Gulf, and Al Khobar, another adjacent town, is where
the majority of the expatriates live. (See map, page 64.) Within an
hour's drive to the north is the coastal industrial town of Jubail and
one of the world's largest refineries at Ras Tanura. Just south of Al
Khobar is the King Fahd Causeway to the island Emirate of
Bahrain. The climate can be moderately humid, but strong winds
often alleviate this in summer. Rain comes between December and
April.

Supermarkets
Tamimi Safeway (selection is more American); Aziziya (mainly British); Giant Stores, Dammam (bulk goods).

Childrens' clothes
Mothercare, BHS (Al Khobar Corniche and Al Rashid Mall), Baby Shop, Dammam.

Adults' clothes
BHS, Next, Benetton, Al Sawani, Al Rashid Mall, Al Khobar Plaza and Al Danah Mall, Dammam.

Toys
Excellent selection (see Chapter 7, 'Toys').

Hobby supplies
Good selection (see Chapter 7, 'Hobbies and sports').

Antiques
Very good selection (see Chapter 7, 'Middle East items').

Restaurants
Al Khobar: Le Gulf Meridien Hotel (864 6000); Carlton Al Moaibed Hotel (Tel: 857 5455, Fax: 857 5433, website: *www.carlton-hotel.com.sa*); Al Sanbok (seafood) (894 8889), La Gondola (Italian) (894 0913); *Dammam*: Sheraton Dammam Hotel & Towers (Tel: 834 5555, Fax: 834 9872).

Car hire
Budget (898 4619; Hanco (894 9002 or toll-free Kingdom-wide 800 304 1111); Hala (894 6316).

Hospitals
Al Mana General, Al Khobar (898 7000); Al Thomairy General, Al Khobar (859 0024); Al Mouwasat, Dammam (0820 000).

Schools
The British School, PO Box 4359, Al Khobar 31952 Tel: 882 5425. Fax: 882 5303. (pre-school up to Year 9 13–14 years old); Dhahran Academy (British Section), PO Box 677, Al Khobar 31952 (Tel: 330 0555 ext. 2003, Fax: 330 2450 ext 2037) pre-school up to Year 11 – 15 years old; Jubail British. (Tel: 341 7550. Fax: 341 6990); Jubail International. (Tel: 341 7550/7681. Fax: 341 6990).

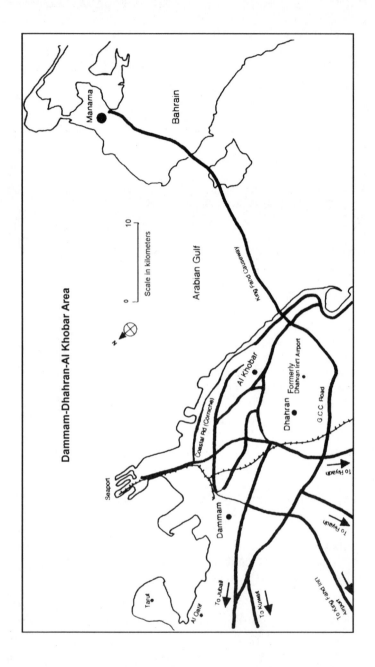

Fig. 9. Map of Dammam/Dhahran/Al Khobar area.

Organisations
Numerous social and business organisations; contact the British Trade Office (Tel: 882 5300. Fax: 882 5384. Email: *btokhobar @hotmail.com*) for details. The British Businessmen's Association. (Tel: 882 5288 ext. 1443. Fax: 882 5384).

Activities
Tennis, squash, softball, soccer and rugby are all played competitively. Diving and snorkelling in the Arabian Gulf are popular water sports; some windsurfing and sailing is also possible. There are a few private beaches, but unless you are an employee of the owner, access is by invitation only.

Travel
Nearby Bahrain is accessible by car on the Causeway, but you need an exit/re-entry visa to visit. There are direct flights to Singapore daily. Thailand, Kenya and the Maldives are also popular destinations. The United Arab Emirates, Qatar and Kuwait are within driving distance, or a short flight away.

Jubail
In the 1970s the Royal Commission began two major construction projects; the building of two industrial cities, Jubail on the Arabian Gulf, and Yanbu on the Red Sea. The result is 120 industrial plants, with more on the drawing boards. Before construction of the two cities began, environmental concerns were targeted to prevent destruction of wildlife habitats and archaeological areas. Environmental impact assessments were made in order to study the impact of rapid industrialisation on the ecosystem. Due to its regard for the environment, and careful planning, the Royal Commission has received international awards for its environmental programmes.

The old city of Jubail is quite small and shopping is limited. For this reason shoppers head for Al Khobar or Dammam, a one-hour drive away. Due to its rapid growth, housing is in demand and several new housing areas are under construction. Currently, the majority of Jubail's residents live in an integrated neighbour setting. There are approximately twenty-three nationalities represented in Jubail. Unfortunately many of the new housing areas are compound style. Many in Jubail are sorry to see the neighbourhood setting disappear. Along with housing, shopping malls are also under construction to meet the needs of this growing population. The Royal Commission has a wonderful museum with displays describing

Grid No.	Compound name	GridNo.	Compound Name
C-5 1.	Al Bilad	D-6 45.	Jawhara/Riyadh 'B'/BAe
D-5 2.	Al Bilad II	D-5 46.	Juffali
D-5 3.	Al Bustan	E-6 47.	J&P
E-5 4.	Al Dana/BAe	C-5 48.	Kanoo
D-5 5.	Al Derbas	E-6 49.	KFU
E-6 6.	Al Dossary	D-7 50.	KFUPM
D-7 7.	Al Ferdous	B-7 51.	Lotus/BAe
E-5 8.	Al Gosaibi/BAe	F-6 52.	Meridian Village
D-5 9.	Al Hada	C-6 53.	Monopoly Village
D-6 10.	Al Khobar Garden Vil./BAe	D-7 54.	MD3
D-6 11.	Al Khobar Gardens/BAe	D-6 55.	MD5
D-3 12.	Al Khodari	D-7 56.	MD9
E-5 13.	Al Khozama Al Corniche	D-7 57.	MD 16/Riyadh 'A'
D-4 14.	Al Khozama Flower/BAe	E-4 58.	MD 18/Al Rakah
D-3 15.	Al Kuhaimi Villas	F-2 59.	MD 22/Jadawel City
C-6 16.	Al Mouhawis/BAe	D-5 60.	MD/The Motel
C-3 17.	Al Mutlaq	D-5 61.	NCB
E-5 18.	Al Nada	D-5 62.	Oasis/Soha
C-4 19.	Al Nakheel	D-5 63.	Oasis/Mishal
D-5 20.	Al Qadisiyah	D-6 64.	Okal/BAe
D-3 21.	Al Qahtani	D-5 65.	Red Sea
D-6 22.	Al Rowdha/BAe	D-5 66.	Rezayat Village
D-4 23.	Al Rimaih	E-5 67.	R.O.C. Villas
D-5 24.	Al Rushaid I	C-5 68.	Rolaco
D-5 25.	Al Rushaid II	D-3 69.	Saipem
D-8 26.	Al Rushaid III	A-6 70.	Saudi Aramco
E-4 27.	Al Saeed I & II	D-4 71.	Saudi French Bank
E-5 28.	Al Salam	C-1 72.	Saudi Naval Base
E-5 29.	Al Suwaiket	E-6 73.	Seaview/BAe
D-5 30.	Al Zahra	C-5 74.	SSOC
C-3 31.	Al Zamil	C-3 75.	Stadium/BAe
E-3 32.	APICORP	C-5 76.	Steidle
C-5 33.	Arabian Village	D-5 77.	STEMCO
E-6 34.	ASEA	E-9 78.	SWCC
E-3 35.	ATCO	D-5 79.	Tamimi
D-5 36.	Canary Village	E-5 80.	Tamimi
C-4 37.	CCC	D-5 81.	TASECO
D-5 38.	Dresser Atlas	D-5 82.	Thomson
D-5 39.	E.T.E.	C-5 83.	TIG
E-5 40.	Eurovillage	B-6 84.	TRADCO
C-5 41.	Fluor	B-7 85.	USMTM
E-6 42.	Gama I	B-6 86.	US Consulate
C-3 43.	Gama II	E-9 84.	Waha
E-3 44.	Golden Belt	D-7 88.	3D/I

Fig. 10. Al Khobar compound map.

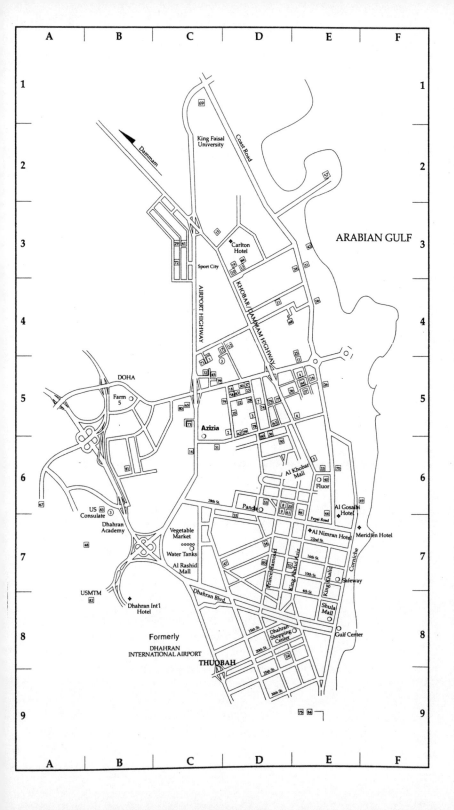

the formidable construction of Jubail. Reservations are required. The climate is similar to the Dammam/Al Khobar area.

Supermarkets
None. Women drive to Al Khobar for the major grocery shopping. There are vegetable, fruit and fish markets, also small grocery stores for basics.

Clothing
Very limited. Shoppers buy in Al Khobar or on home leave.

Toys
Purchase in Dammam or Al Khobar.

Hobby supplies
Purchase in Dammam or Al Khobar.

Antiques
Good selection of Arabic brass, copper and jewellery.

Restaurants
The Dhow (a converted ship); Holiday Inn; fast food and local.

Hospitals
A full service hospital and clinic with a good reputation.

School
Jubail British Academy, PO Box 10059, Madinat Al Jubail Al Sinaiyah 31961. Tel: (03) 341 7550. Fax: (03) 341 6990.

Organisations
Women's club.

Activities
All water sports available. The Holiday Inn offers a Beach Club for Westerners. There are many arts and crafts, cooking, sewing, quilting, painting, language and computer classes available. The list of activities is extensive and those listed are only a sampling.

Travel
The nearest airport is (Dammam) King Fahd International Airport, 45 minutes' drive from Al Khobar. A taxi costs approximately SR 90 one way.

CASE STUDY

A family choose to live off-compound

A British family in Al Khobar were given a housing allowance of SR 40,000 p.a. by their company. They found that the standard of accommodation available on compounds within their price range was disappointing. By driving around they picked an area of town they liked and talked to several estate agents in the area. They found a three-bedroomed semi-detached villa with a small swimming pool for SR 40,000 a year. Decoratively, it was in rough condition when they took it and they have done extensive work to bring it up to their own standards.

The wife says she did spend a lot of time waiting around for lifts to get to places, but also says her husband worked close by and was willing to help out daily with school runs, *etc.* It suited her to be away from compound gossip, but sometimes they were bothered by the neighbours keeping unsociable hours.

DISCUSSION POINTS

1. Your compound will very much be your world. Do you prefer variety, or do you feel comfortable socialising with the same small group of people every day?

2. Do you like participating in, or organising, events for your neighbourhood?

3. Do you mind living close to, and socialising, in a group with work colleagues?

4

Doing Business

OBSERVING CUSTOMS AND ETIQUETTE

Office protocol

Entering a Saudi businessman's office may be a bit overwhelming on your first visit. During your meeting there may be several interruptions. Other businessmen or employees may enter the office to seek advice or they may be making a courtesy call. You may be ushered into an office that is filled with people.

It is a Saudi tradition to have an 'open door' policy. Join in the conversation, but do not bring up specific business questions, as this would be considered rude. As negotiations proceed and confidentiality is required, private meetings will take place. Until that time arrives your business will be discussed openly and publicly.

'Space'

When introduced to a Saudi, or speaking with a Saudi, you will be aware of their close proximity to you. 'Space' is a Western concept. Try not to step back as the Saudi will think of it as a rebuff.

Gestures

Saudis are 'touchers' when they talk, but not back-slappers. We Westerners have a tendency to use our hands when we speak, using broad, wide gestures. Refrain from using such gestures as it is considered impolite. Also, beckoning or pointing with your finger is considered insulting.

The sole of your shoe

When a man sits he quite often crosses his leg, with his ankle resting on his knee. In this position the sole of the shoe is exposed. The sole of your shoe should never face a Saudi, it is extremely insulting. By exposing the sole of your shoe to a Saudi you are saying, in effect, 'you are less than dirt'.

Language
Saudis do not appreciate loud, boisterous behaviour. Swearing, crude language, referring to any Saudi in derogatory terms, such as 'you idiot', is highly offensive. Never use the name of an animal when referring to a child or adult, such as 'what a little monkey'. Dignity (often referred to as 'face') is very important to the Saudis. If you offend a Saudi, you have offended his entire family.

Making entrances and exits
Saudis enter a room according to rank; the highest ranking enters first. When Saudis greet each other it is with a kiss on each cheek; with Westerners they shake hands. At the completion of the meeting always escort the Saudi to the door. When at home, escort your guests to their cars. This courtesy will be reciprocated.

Exchanging business cards
When introduced to a Saudi, business cards are exchanged. Your card should be printed in both English and Arabic; present the Arabic side face up to the Saudi. Business cards become your address and phone book as many numbers are unlisted.

A right-handed society
Once introductions have taken place Arabic coffee or tea will be served. Politeness requires you to drink one cup, but never more than three. To indicate you have finished drinking, either wiggle the cup back and forth, or cover the cup with your hand. Always accept food or drink with your *right hand*. The right hand is also used when accepting or giving papers, documents, gifts or money. The left hand is used for hygienic functions.

Building trust
You may attend many business meetings where business is not discussed and may feel you are wasting your time. You are not. At this time the Saudi is taking your measure, noting your competence and knowledge of your product or service. He is also determining your trustworthiness. A Saudi business relationship is based on trust; without it, there is no business agreement.

Gift-giving
Gift-giving takes place after contractual negotiations have been completed, never before, as this could be construed as a bribe and your Saudi counterpart will be highly insulted.

In a social situation it is not necessary to bring a gift for your host, although a small gift is considered as a courteous gesture. If you know the family well you may bring flowers; if you do not know the family, do not bring flowers as this is an insult to the husband and shows familiarity with his wife. For this reason you should not give a gift specifically for your host's wife. Gifts for the children of your host are acceptable and welcome.

You may be invited to the wedding celebration of a member of a Saudi colleague's family and not know the bride or groom. In this case a gift is not expected. Close friends and family members give gifts a few days after the night of the wedding celebration.

Gifts may also be given during *Ramadan, Eid* and *Haj.* At the time of *Ramadan* food and fruit are given. At *Eid* sweets are acceptable. During *Haj* gifts are given to children.

Accepting and giving invitations

Quite often Saudis invite their guests on very short notice, and there is a ritual to accepting a verbal invitation. Politely refuse once or twice, and then graciously accept. Always arrive on time. Saudi couples frequently entertain separately. Discreetly inquire if your host includes your wife in the invitation.

When you invite a Saudi to your home he will politely refuse; persist a few more times, as is the custom. Many Saudi wives do not attend male/female functions. The Saudi husband may accept the invitation for his wife, but do not be offended if she does not attend.

Making conversation

Polite and prolonged conversation takes place before the meal is served. Never discuss business at a social gathering, unless initiated by your host, or you may be considered rude and discourteous. It will also seriously affect any future business arrangements. Enquiring about the host and his family is expected, but do so generally, do not be too specific and do not ask about his wife, unless you know the family quite well. When admiring an item in your host's home do not become too enthusiastic with praise or your host will feel obliged to offer the item to you.

Going to dinner

The invitation may read 'dinner at 8'. but the dinner may not be served until 10 pm after prolonged conversation. There may be little conversation taking place during dinner, as the Saudis enjoy their meal. Your host will present a sumptuous meal; always leave a small amount of food on your plate, this will assure your host that he has provided more than enough food for his guests. Guests leave after the presentation of incense or shortly after the meal has finished.

UNDERSTANDING THE BUSINESS CLIMATE

Diversification and privatisation
The volatile oil market of the 1980s and the high cost of the Gulf War in the early 1990s resulted in a reduction of government spending. The Saudi government hopes to achieve economic stability with a two-pronged approach. First, to decrease its dependence on oil revenue through diversification by developing industry, agriculture and mining. Second, through privatisation such as joint ventures with foreign companies. This new business philosophy will create many new opportunities for industries and service related companies inside, as well as outside, the oil sector.

The collapse of oil prices in 1998 and early 1999 had a negative impact on the country's economy but GDP growth of 5.1 per cent is expected for 2000, assuming oil prices remain favourable.

Saudization
The future of the Kingdom of Saudi Arabia is in the Saudization of the private sector, ARAMCO and SABIC affiliates, in order to achieve a stable and viable economy. Simply put, Saudization is the integration of the Saudi people into all aspects of the workforce. Saudi Arabia has one of the world's highest population growth rates. One out of five Saudis is unemployed, and fifty per cent of its population is under the age of 15. The Saudi government has instituted a programme aimed at training and employing this very large future workforce. In December 1995 Resolution 50 was decreed. This decree requires the private sector to increase its Saudi staff by five per cent a year. Many jobs that were once filled by expat workers have already gone to Saudi workers. With the creation of the Supreme Economic Council in 1999 the pace of change is expected to pick up.

Changes to rules governing foreign investment in Saudi Arabia are being considered as are changes to the country's tax code. At present taxes on foreign businesses range as high as forty-five per cent. Foreign ownership rules may also change. Currently foreigners are allowed to own up to forty-nine per cent of any joint venture, need a Saudi sponsor, and are not allowed to own property. In late

1999 international investors were permitted to invest in local shares through established open-ended mutual funds.

Job opportunities with Saudization
During this time of transition many new job opportunities have been created. Job training has become a major focus within the business community. This includes the transfer of technology. Companies offering training programmes, software for training programmes, and consultants to initiate and teach programmes, are in high demand.

Knowing where to start

Ask any successful businessman in Saudi Arabia how to begin and maintain a viable working relationship with his Saudi counterpart and he begins a discourse on 'The Ps'. They are listed below; each one is equally important.

- **Positive**. Maintain a positive attitude. This may not be as easy as it sounds. You will confront many business and cultural differences that you must adjust to.

- **Prudent**. Know your market, and know your agent (see Selecting an Agent, below). Do not become involved in a contract until you are aware of all the liabilities.

- **Patience**. Many changes have taken place in Saudi Arabia and the *look* is very modern, but these are surface changes. The Saudis are conservative by tradition and culture. Also, during the 'boom' years many unscrupulous businessmen took advantage of a (then) naïve business community. The Saudi decision-making process is slow. From the beginning of negotiations to actual start-up can take years. When planning your business venture this factor should be given serious consideration.

- **Presence**. Your presence within the Kingdom is very important. Sending letters and faxes is not acceptable, and sending a subordinate in your place is a major no-no. In the case of large companies the Saudis expect representation from senior management. The Saudis want to be assured of your commitment to the business venture and that it will result in a *long-term relationship*.

- **Perspective**. If all of this appears to be rather daunting at times, keep in mind your objectives and goals. And do not hesitate to ask for help. The end result, or bottom-line, will justify the effort involved.

MARKETING

Before you sign a formal agreement investigate the market possibilities and the company you plan to be associated with. A service or product that sells well in Dubai may not be marketable or feasible in Saudi Arabia, or the market may be saturated with similar companies firmly established in the Kingdom.

Marketing help from the UK
A good place to begin your enquiries is at the Saudi Desk of the Department of Trade and Industry, or your local Government Office or Business Link. They have professional staff to help and can provide invaluable information. Their range of services includes the following:

- Advice on doing business in Saudi Arabia.

- Advice on appointing a local agent.

- Market information enquiries. These can help to provide customised local contact lists, give an assessment of the market for a product or service, advice on market approach, provide a list of potential local agents/distributors, supply status information on local contacts (*not* credit checks). These enquiries, commissioned through the government offices and Business Links, are chargeable at a rate depending on the number of man hours involved.

- Major project information.

- Free off-the-shelf lists: interpreters/translators, lawyers, accountants, banks, conference organisers.

- Exhibition and trade mission support. It is often invaluable to make a first visit to the market with a sponsored Trade Mission, which gives official support and more focus and publicity to individual company activities.

Marketing help from Saudi Arabia

- Saudi Chamber of Commerce has a broad range of information. They have offices throughout the Kingdom. All registered companies must become members of the Chamber if they are involved in importing, exporting, or bidding for government contracts.

- Saudi Consulting House conducts market and feasibility studies for a fee.

- Saudi Industrial Development Fund (SIDF) provides marketing, financial and technical advice along with loans for joint venture projects.

- Saudi Arabian Standards Organisation sets the standards for products and processes to be used on a project.

SELECTING AN AGENT OR SPONSOR

Begin your association through correspondence and visits to the Kingdom. Do not rush this procedure. The Saudi Chamber of Commerce emphasises the importance of developing a strong working relationship with your Saudi counterpart. They equate this relationship to a marriage and suggest a long courtship. As in all courtships the suitor must be present. Your agent or sponsor wants to build a relationship based on trust, with the knowledge that your company intends to stay in the Kingdom.

The Saudi Chamber of Commerce warns potential businessmen to the Kingdom to be aware of unscrupulous agents or sponsors and lawyers. The Saudi Chamber of Commerce wants foreign business-men to have a successful and profitable relationship with their Saudi counterparts. In order to achieve this goal investigate the credibility and financial position of your future agent through the Saudi Chamber of Commerce and the British Trade Office. They will lead you to other sources of information. To quote a Saudi Chamber of Commerce Officer, 'getting a divorce is easier than breaking your contract with an agent'.

Agencies are divided into two groups:

- The **commercial agent** is a term covering both agencies and distributorships.

- **Service agencies** are necessary for foreign contractors or consultants who do not have a Saudi partner and who wish to participate in Saudi government contracts.

Using commercial agencies
Selling to the private sector from *outside* Saudi Arabia does not require an agent. But if you intend to make more than the occasional sale, or you want someone to market and sell your product from within the Kingdom, a Saudi agent or distributorship will be necessary.

All government purchasing is conducted by local tender and only Saudi companies may bid. Therefore, foreign companies will need an agent or distributorship who will represent them for the bidding process.

Regulations for commercial agencies
Commercial agencies are controlled by Royal Decree No. M/11 of 1962 as amended by Royal Decree No. M/5 of 1969 and No. M/32 of 1980, Ministry of Commerce Resolution No. 1897 of 1981, Council of Ministers Resolution 124 of 1980.

All commercial agencies must be registered with the Ministry of Commerce.

The agreement signed between the agency and foreign company is a contract and legally binding. Therefore, the rights and responsibilities of each party need to be precisely defined.

Commercial agency agreements are reviewed by the Ministry of Commerce before registration. Any essential elements that are excluded from the agreement will result in the rejection of the agreement by the Ministry.

In May 1983 the Ministry developed a model form of a commercial agency/distributorship contract which was amended by 1988. Because this is a model form contract both parties involved in the contract may amend the contract to suit their particular needs, but the essential elements of the model contract must be met. To ensure all legal requirements have been met legal advice should be obtained.

All agency agreements between Saudi agents and foreign companies are subject to Saudi law. The Ministry of Commerce does not allow disputes to be argued outside the jurisdiction of Saudi courts. The Ministry will consider a clause allowing for arbitration of disputes outside the Kingdom.

Termination of a commercial agency agreement
Terminating an agency or distributorship contract is very difficult. Terms for termination should be clearly defined, including the duration of the contract. Under the Ministry of Commerce model contract form, either party who has sustained damages by unjustified termination or non-renewal of the contract may claim compensation from the other party. Also, the Ministry has a policy that no new commercial agency may be registered while there is an ongoing dispute. If the dissolution of the contract is not amicable it may be difficult to find a Saudi company willing to take on the agency. 'Agent hopping' is definitely discouraged.

What the commercial agent (or distributorship) provides for your company
- Knowledge of local laws, regulations and customs which affect business.

- Back-up and servicing facilities, including qualified personnel (under the new official format of a model contract supplied by the Ministry of Commerce, you, as principal, will be required to develop as necessary).

- Storage facilities that are available for equipment and spare parts.

- Ability to import and stock inventory in order to supply goods, products, *etc* upon customer demand.

- Ability to cover the sales and distribution territory effectively. Few agents are able to provide the expertise and manpower to operate effectively in all three main trading centres of Riyadh, Jeddah and the Eastern Province. For this reason, be aware of what service your agent is capable of providing. In order to cover the entire Kingdom you may require an agent for each area. Also, some agents will not be able to service all of your products. Under Saudi Law you may appoint agents on a regional basis and for particular products. You may also restrict the coverage of an agency. *Your contract should clearly state which area of the Kingdom the agent will service and what produce lines they will distribute.*

- Visas, local transport, driver's licence, accommodation, appointments, *etc.*

What the foreign partner provides the commercial agent (or distributorship)

- A knowledgeable and experienced sales staff. If the sales staff is not based in the Kingdom then frequent visits are required to maintain a good relationship with the agent and help the local staff market the products.

- Short training visits to the UK for salesmen and maintenance personnel from within the agent's staff.

- The main sales effort. There are more foreign firms than there are established agents. For this reason many firms place a sales representative within the Saudi company to market their product.

- Up-to-date technical and pricing information. There are often short deadlines for bidding in Saudi Arabia. It is essential that the agent is kept informed of the latest product information and that questions are answered promptly.

Using service agencies

A foreign contractor who does not have a Saudi partner must apply for a temporary licence from the Ministry of Commerce within thirty days of signing a Saudi government contract, and have a copy of the agreement with the Saudi service agent in order to enter into the government contract.

A consultant must have a Saudi service agent who is a Saudi consultant.

Regulations for services agencies

Service agencies are controlled by Royal Decree No. M/2 of 1978. A service agent may represent up to ten foreign contractors. A service agent receives a commission not to exceed five per cent.

TYPES OF PARTNERSHIP

Legal aspects in the formation of partnerships

All business and company entities are regulated by Companies Law under Royal Decrees issued in 1965, and amended in 1982 and 1992. Under Article 1 of the Companies Law:

'A company has been defined as a contract pursuant to which each of two or more persons undertake to participate, in an enterprise aiming at profit, by offering in specie or as work a share, for sharing in the profits or losses resulting from such enterprise.'

Also:

'With the exception of joint ventures, any company incorporated in accordance with these Regulations shall establish its head office in the Kingdom. It shall be deemed to have Saudi nationality, but this shall not necessarily entail its enjoyment of such rights as may be restricted to Saudis.'

Additionally:

- Regardless of the type of partnership agreement entered into, all companies must be registered with the Ministry of Commerce.

- Upon registration the company acquires its own legal identity, unless it is a joint venture.

- Information must be supplied in the statutes of the company, such as: type of company, its objectives, location of head office, financial data, *etc.*

- Contractual conditions of the partnership must meet the requirements of the Regulations for Companies.

- The partnership is dissolved if one individual owns all of the shares or interest in the company.

General partnerships

General partnerships are defined as two or more persons that are jointly liable for the partnership debts. As a legal entity it can transact business under its own name and does not require a minimum capital investment. The contribution requirement for each partner is stipulated in the partnership agreement. General partnerships are set up by Saudi nationals.

Joint ventures, limited liability partnerships and limited partnerships

Within Saudi Arabia joint ventures are usually a limited liability partnership or a limited partnership with a foreign partner. Joint ventures are usually entered into for industrial, agricultural, contracting and services projects. Oversight, and the issuing of licences for joint ventures, is controlled by the Ministry of Industry and Electricity. The time required for the issuing of licences and registration of the company is six months. The requirements for joint ventures are:

- Obtaining a Foreign Capital Investment Licence.

- Agreement between the foreign and Saudi partners on the terms of the project.

- The Saudi partner is identified by the foreign partner.

- A shareholders' agreement is drawn up.

- The Saudi partner must obtain approval for the project from the Ministry of Industry and Electricity.

- A feasibility study with detailed information on the project is submitted to the Ministry of Industry and Electricity and the Foreign Capital Investment Committee.

- An application is submitted to the above ministries with detailed information, including financial statements. The application must be in Arabic.

- The Foreign Capital Investment Committee makes its recommendations to the Ministry of Industry and Electricity, which will issue a Foreign Capital Investment Licence.

- The joint venture partners submit the company's articles of association to the Ministry of Commerce for approval, which are then notarised and published in the Official Gazette.

- A bank account is opened and a certificate is submitted to the Ministry of Commerce, which issues a commercial registration number.

- With the registration of the company the partners may apply for financing.

INVESTMENT WITH INCENTIVES

Financing
Although many projects continue to be funded through revenues from oil, the Saudis are trying to break away from government financing of projects. Several different financial tools are in use to reach the private investment sector.

Investment organisations

The Saudi stock exchange
Once launched, many projects that originated with government funds are handed over to the private sector through the Saudi stock exchange for private investing. Although this is not an official stock exchange, the banks have set up a network for dealing with joint stock companies, with publicly traded shares, which is controlled by the Saudi Arabian Monetary Agency (SAMA). Trading is open to Saudi citizens. The only exceptions are GCC nationals, whose investment is limited to a few joint stock companies such as SABIC.

– *SAMA* (Saudi Arabian Monetary Agency) is the Kingdom's central bank. It regulates and monitors commercial banks and acts as the government's bank.

– *SABIC* (Saudi Arabian Basic Industries Corporation) promotes and funds joint venture projects in petrochemicals and other oil related industries.

– *NIC* (National Industrialisation Company) is a holding company to encourage private-sector development through new industrial projects.

– *SIDF* (Saudi Industrial Development Fund) provides inexpensive medium- and long-term funds for industrial joint venture projects. They also provide marketing, technical and financial advice.

– *SAAB* (Saudi Arabian Agricultural Bank) provides low-cost loans to the agricultural sector.

Private financing for joint venture projects is also available through the banking sector.

The Saudi government is also turning to the private sector to form joint venture, build-operate-transfer (BOT) and build-to-own (BTO) projects. Through SABIC many successful joint ventures have been completed in Jubail and Yanbu. Foreign companies (with Saudi partners) have set up and are operating manufacturing plants throughout the Kingdom. With these successes the Saudis are actively promoting business development projects through the private sector.

Recently the Saudi government received bond ratings from Moody's and Standard and Poor's. The Saudis are hopeful that in the future they will be able to fund some projects through the international bond market.

Saudi Arabia has joined the World Trade Organization and will be a full member within ten years.

Paying taxes

All companies operating in Saudi Arabia are required to submit an income tax or *zakat* return each year to the Department of Zakat and Income Tax. A local accountant should be consulted for tax advice. The Ministry of Finance and National Economy, Directorate of Zakat and Income, Companies Department will also help answer your questions.

There are no taxes on salaries.

Additional incentives

To encourage private sector development the Saudi government is offering many incentives to foreign businesses. As an example, companies in the manufacturing sector are offered the following incentives:

- no currency restrictions (and unlimited movement of capital into or out of the Kingdom)
- low cost of land (purchased through a joint venture)
- soft loans (fifteen-year repayment, two per cent charge)
- ten-year tax holiday
- products manufactured in-Kingdom given government preference over competing imported foreign products for the supply of its procurement
- no taxes on imported machinery, equipment and raw materials used by industry.

The infrastructure

- superhighways linking all the major cities within the Kingdom
- wells and desalination plants provide water
- electricity is relatively inexpensive
- seaports with latest dock facilities
- airports at all major cities provides in-Kingdom service.

Using communications

The telecommunications sector in Saudi Arabia is going through a period of rapid development. In 1998 the Saudi Government took the first steps towards privatising the telecoms industry, and the

Saudi Telecommunications Company (STC) was set-up.

The fibre-optic system has still not been installed. STC is currently working on Telephone Expansion Plan 8 (TEP8) which will create a further 2.2m telephone lines including switchwear, fibre-optic cables, wireless loops, intelligent networks and micro-wave transmissions. Bids from 5 major international contractors have already been submitted.

Services available are:

- *Cellular phones*: Whilst in the past usage was very limited to in-Kingdom, some subscribers can now easily get cellular phone with international acces via worldwide satellite connections.

- *Internet*: True Internet access in Saudi Arabia has become a reality since 1999. Some Internet service providers are listed below.

Al Alamiah Internet & Communications Company
Website: *www.anet.net/sa/*. Email: *mail@anet.net.sa*

ArabNet.SA.
Website: *www.arab.net.sa/*. Email: *webmaster@arab.net.sa.*

AwalNet
Website: *www.awalnet.net.sa/*. Email: *sales@awalnet.net.sa*

Dallah Media Production
Website: *www.dmp.net.sa/*. Email: *services@dmp.net.sa*

Gulfnet KSA – (Zajil)
Website: *www.zajil.net/*. Email: *zajil@zajil.net*

Naseej
Website: *www.naseej.com.sa..* Email: *info@naseej.com.sa*

Nesma
Website: *www.nesma.net.sa/*. Email: *info@nesma.net.sa.*

PrimeNet
Website: *www.prime.net.sa/*. Email: *sales@prime.net.sa.*

Sahara Network
Website: *www.sahara.com.ysa/*. Email: *sales@sahara.com.ysa.*

Saudi Business Machines
Website: *www.sbm.net.sa/*. Email: *inquiry@sbm.net.ysa*

Saudi On Line
Website: *www.saudionline.com.ysa/*.
Email: *marketing@saudionline.com.sa.*

Shabakah Net
Website: *www.shabakah.net.ysa/*. Email: *shakeeb@shabakah.com.*

Shaheer Net
Website: *www.shaheer.net.sa/*. Email: *webmaster@shaheer.net.sa*.
Suhuf
Website: *www.suhuf.net.sa/*. Email: *info@suhuf.net.sa*
- Faxes.

Using the mail
- The post office. Posting mail and pick-up is generally handled through your office, personal mail is billed (stamps, cost of mailing packages) to the employee.
- Pouch or courier system. Most companies have a mail pouch for official business purposes.
- DHL, FedEx, UPS.

Note: phone lines, letters and packages are subject to censorship.

CASE STUDY

An expatriate takes beef to the barbeque
An expatriate is invited by a customer to a pot-luck barbeque at a remote worksite in the Eastern Province. Asked to purchase meat in town for the barbeque, the expatriate goes to a Western style supermarket in Al Khobar and buys some Irish beef steaks. When he arrives and hands the meat over to the barbeque chef at the fire, he notices that a Saudi colleague is handing the cook some chicken. The expatriate explains he has brought a treat of steaks from town. The Saudi politely explains that although the beef was sold in the local supermarket, it was not *halal* (slaughtered according to Islamic law) and therefore he could not eat it, so to avoid embarrassment he always comes prepared with halal chicken for himself.

DISCUSSION POINTS

1. Are you flexible enough to adapt to the Arabic way of doing business?
2. Is your company aware of the difficulties of operating in a different cultural environment?
3. Can you depend on your company to provide a reliable support system?
4. Do you have a good working relationship with your sponsor/ agent?

5

Labour and Legal Matters

CHECKING YOUR PERSONAL AGREEMENT (CONTRACT)

The **personal agreement** is the **contract** between you and your company. It specifies the salary and benefits you are entitled to. It will be the most important document you sign. *Read it very carefully.* Every personal agreement is different and is dependent on the contract your company has signed with the client. Be sure your contract complies with the local labour law and endeavour to ascertain, in advance, your rights under the law.

Married status personal agreements
The following sample agreement is for **married status** employees and should include the following:

- job description
- length of contract
- number of work days (usually stated in the number of hours to be worked each week)
- salary, overtime, bonuses, paid sick leave, paid holidays, paid emergency home leave
- airfare tickets for you and your family (stating category of tickets: first, business, economy)
- excess baggage allowance
- costs incurred for entry into Saudi Arabia for you and your family (passports, visas, photos, medical exams and tests, Saudi driver's licence, *etc*)
- housing to be provided by the company (in some cases a housing allowance may be given; see Chapter 3)
- furnished housing (get specifics so you can pack the appropriate items you will need during your stay; see Chapter 3)
- weight allowance for household goods
- type of shipping: sea or air
- insurance for household goods shipment (check type of insurance, *ie* full replacement value)

- storage and insurance costs for goods not shipped to Saudi Arabia (check if there are any exclusions such as cars, motorbikes, boats)
- insurance (medical, life, accident)
- medical care (check what type of medical care is provided, under what circumstances your company will pay for medical treatment outside KSA and if this includes airfare)
- car and costs of maintaining car (petrol, maintenance, insurance; check if this is your private car or will you be required to share)
- school fees
- boarding school fees for children over 15 (this includes airfare for child to return to KSA for holidays)
- annual holiday (check number of days allotted and if travel days are added onto your annual holiday leave)
- annual holiday round-trip airfare tickets for you and your family.

Some personal agreements may include the following:
- hotel and food allowance for annual holiday
- school books for child attending boarding school
- increase in weight allowance for household goods at end of job assignment
- cost of living allowance.

Single status personal agreements

Many of the terms listed in the personal agreement for a married status employee are valid for a **single status** employee with the following exceptions:

- shipping of household goods and all items related to household goods
- school fees and all items related to schooling
- annual holiday; usually a single status agreement allows for three short-term (generally two weeks) breaks during the year, with airfare for each holiday included.

Recently a few companies are allowing single status employees to bring their spouse with them, but the employee only receives the benefits of a single status employee. All costs for the spouse are paid for by the employee. The company arranges for, and procures, all documentation required by the Saudi government.

Direct hire personal agreements

Those who are employed by a local Saudi company, government office, university, or hospital should make sure their agreements include the terms of the agreements listed above. Beware of a clause (or accompanying letter referring to your personal agreement) within the agreement which allows the Saudi entity to alter or delete any of the terms of the agreement.

MEDICAL BENEFITS

General Organisation of Social Insurance (GOSI)

GOSI is a medical scheme provided by the government, but paid into by all employers and employees. Employers pay nine per cent of the employee's monthly base salary, and employees pay five per cent of their monthly base salary. All employers are required by law to register their employees with GOSI. Money is paid out to an employee who is seriously injured in a job-related accident which prevents him from working. Dependants are exempt from GOSI benefits. GOSI benefits are currently under review by the Ministry of Finance.

Medical insurance

Unfortunately the days of free health care for expats are gone. Today all private-sector companies provide health insurance for their employees. Under the new programme companies pay eighty per cent of an employee's health care benefits and the employee is responsible for twenty per cent. Each company has its own health care package. Generally, a company signs an agreement with a specific hospital which has a clinic offering a full range of medical services. The services provided by the clinic usually include:

- general practitioner
- specialists: orthopaedics, cardiology, obstetrics, *etc.*
- paediatrics
- maternity
- eye care
- dental care
- physical therapy.

Be sure you know what type of coverage you are entitled to. Your medical insurance package may not pay for all of the services provided by the clinic. If you are dissatisfied with the service provided by the clinic or hospital you may go to any private clinic or hospital of your choosing, but your insurance may not pay the fees. Please note: some private hospitals are only for Saudi nationals.

Although your company provides health insurance coverage while in the Kingdom, it may not cover you and your family when you travel outside of the Kingdom. Make sure you are covered before you travel.

LEGAL AND LABOUR ISSUES

There are four very important facts to know:

1. The British Embassy/Consulate is unable to intervene if you or your employee or their dependants break Saudi law. (For details see Functions of the British Embassy/Consulates below.)

2. The Embassy/Consulates are unable to intervene in contractual or labour disputes. According to the booklet *Living in Saudi Arabia, A Brief Guide*, provided by the Consular Department, Foreign and Commonwealth Office, March 1994:

   'The 1969 Labour and Workmen Law is administered by the local Labour Offices who adjudicate in any dispute between contracting parties... Aggrieved employees are generally advised to settle, if at all possible, directly with their employer without recourse to the labour office, where the procedures can be lengthy and legal costs high. (Direct settlement with the employer can also help in avoiding problems over the eventual exit visa, for which only the employer can apply, and over accommodation)... If you break (your contract) for any reason you may find that your employer will not provide you with the letter of release (No Objection Certificate) which is necessary to enable you to work for another organisation in the country. Bear in mind that you will probably have to pay your homeward fare (as well as on occasion recruitment and other related costs) so it is important to remain at work until you have earned enough money (to pay for these costs)... If you are in Saudi Arabia as the employee of a British company which has won a contract there, it may seem that "sponsorship" does not apply to you. It does: the only difference is the direct relationship of responsibility is between your British firm and its Saudi sponsor.'

3. The employer (company) is also the sponsor for all employees and the dependants of employees. Any costs or damages incurred by an employee, or the employee's dependants, is the

financial responsibility of the company. *As the company representative you can be held personally responsible for company debts.*

4. As an employee your company and/or sponsor is legally responsible for you. They will provide you with all the legal documentation that is required. *But if you break the law their responsibility ceases.* If you break the law you will not be given special treatment because you are a foreign worker. Saudi punishment for breaking the law is severe. Your sentence could result in fines, a jail term, lashes and deportation. If you are deported from Saudi Arabia you will not be allowed to re-enter the Kingdom with another company or sponsor. Most companies will either supply you with a lawyer or provide a list to choose from, at your cost. Generally, if you are imprisoned the company will send a representative to ensure you receive the same treatment as other prisoners, but they cannot insist on special treatment. Realise your company/sponsor is not required by law to provide these services for you.

Contracts and documents are written in the Arabic language
All legal documents (royal degrees, laws, contracts, *etc*) are written in the Arabic language. This document is considered to be the legally binding instrument which will be referred to in any legal dispute. For this reason it behoves the businessman to engage the services of a highly qualified Arabic translator.

Arabic (Hejira) calendar vs. Gregorian calendar
All documents and contracts are dated according to the *Hejira* calendar. Generally, contracts will have the Gregorian calendar date written in parentheses following the *Hejira* calendar date. The *Hejira* calendar year consists of twelve lunar months which are one or two days shorter than those in the Gregorian calendar. It is important to keep this in mind when having your visa reissued.

Drugs and alcohol
Most offences committed by expatriates involve alcohol. Sentences vary from a few weeks to several months in jail for consumption of alcohol. If you are smuggling, manufacturing or distributing alcohol the sentence could be several years in prison. Lashes may also be included in your sentence.

The mandatory sentence for drug-smuggling in Saudi Arabia is death. Possession of even the smallest amounts of a drug can lead to a lengthy prison term. *If you are taking medication make sure you carry your prescription with you when entering or leaving the Kingdom.* Medications have been taken for analysis.

Road accidents

Many expatriates become involved in road accidents. The police will take you to the police station and investigate the cause and responsibility for the accident. Notify your company immediately so that they may send a representative to assist you. Normally, the driver(s) held responsible for the accident in which damage or injury has occurred will be imprisoned. The driver(s) will also be responsible for monetary compensation in the case of death, injury or damage. In the case of death, 'blood money' is paid to the relatives. The rate varies.

Legal procedures if arrested

The following information is taken from *Living in Saudi Arabia, A Brief Guide* (Consular Department, Foreign and Commonwealth Office, March 1994)

'The police will question the person arrested and carry out any relevant investigation and require the person to make a statement. The accused may not be allowed the benefit of any outside contact (with employers, friends, consul or lawyer) as long as the investigation continues. If the police decide that there is a case to answer, the accused will be remanded in custody and probably moved from a police station to a prison until he/she can appear before a judge to confirm that the signed statement is accurate and was not made under actual physical duress. Whilst in police custody the Consul (Embassy/Consulate) representative will normally have unrestricted access to the prisoner. However, once the prisoner has been moved to prison the Consul will be granted only limited access. There will then be a further remand in custody until the trial, which the judge will conduct in accordance with Koranic law. There is no jury and, although the accused has no right to a lawyer or Embassy representative, judges can (and sometimes do) permit consular attendance. An interpreter is provided by the court. In the event of a conviction the judge will normally impose a sentence and require the person convicted to sign acceptance of the sentence (unless there is to be an appeal against conviction to a higher court). An appeal can take up to a year to be heard. Occasionally, expatriates may simply be deported after a few days or weeks in police detention, *but this rarely happens.*'

Additional legal facts

- As an employee you must surrender your passport to your

sponsor while you are in the Kingdom. Your company/sponsor will give you identity papers called an *Iqama*, which you must carry with you at all times. Spouses of employees should carry a copy of the employee's *Iqama* for identification purposes.

- It is not possible to enter or exit the Kingdom of Saudi Arabia without an entry or exit visa. Only your company/sponsor can provide this documentation.

- Many companies/sponsors insist upon a letter from the employee stating his wife and children have permission to leave the Kingdom without him. This is a form letter supplied by the company/sponsor. The company/sponsor will not issue an exit visa for the wife and children without this letter.

- Each child should have his/her own passport. If the children are on the wife's passport she may not be allowed out of the Kingdom unless the children are accompanying her.

Additional labour facts

- No Objection Certificate (NOC) is a letter of release from your current employer in Saudi Arabia. Without an NOC you will not be allowed to work for another company in Saudi Arabia.

- There are no trade unions in Saudi Arabia.

- An English translation of the labour laws of Saudi Arabia is available through the Ministry of Labour and Social Affairs. The English translation of labour regulations is for general information only. *The Arabic text is the official text, having full legal force.*

FUNCTIONS OF THE BRITISH EMBASSY/CONSULATES

The main function of an embassy or consulate is to promote a strong diplomatic relationship between the host country and the country represented by the embassy or consulate. This relationship allows both countries an avenue to express their concerns in dealing with one another, hopefully resulting in a mutual understanding of each country's stand on issues as they pertain to them. The second function of the embassy or consulate is the promotion of goods and services from the country they represent.

The British Embassy is located in Riyadh, the capital of Saudi Arabia.

The British Embassy, PO Box 94351, Riyadh 11693, Saudi Arabia. Tel: 01 488 0077. Fax: 01 488 2373.

There is a British Consulate offering full services in Jeddah, located on the west coast of Saudi Arabia.
British Consulate-General, PO Box 393, Jeddah 21411, Saudi Arabia. Tel: 02 654 1811. Fax: 02 654 4917.

There is a Trade Office in Al Khobar, located in the Eastern Province. Tel: 03 882 5300. Fax: 03 882 5384.

Services provided for the expat
There is a great deal of confusion within the expat community regarding what an embassy or consulate can do for the individual expat.

Registering at the embassy or consulate
First, they have to know you are here. It is very important that you and your family register with the embassy or consulate in your area. A **registration** card can be obtained from the reception desk of the embassy/consulate. You should re-register every January and notify them if you have a change of address or are permanently leaving the country.

The offices have a number of booklets and leaflets containing information on living in Saudi Arabia. They are free.

General services
The following is a list of services provided by the embassy and consulate-general in Jeddah. If you are located in the Al Khobar area the Trade Office can provide you with the applications and forward them to the embassy. The average time taken between despatch and return is about two weeks. The timings are based on applications and requests which are correctly made and supported by the necessary documentation. They can advise you on what is required and the consular fees charged for these services.

Service	Average time taken to complete in Riyadh (working days)
Issue/renewal of passport	5 days
Registration of birth	5 days
Registration of death	3 days

Notarial acts (certifying copies and translations, swearing of oaths, witnessing signatures, *etc*)	1 day (or where an appointment has been made, the same day)
Marriage at the embassy	(please ask the counter staff for more details)

Protective work
- If arrested: Visit you in custody as soon as possible after notification of arrest; provide a list of local lawyers; give advice on local procedures; liaise with sponsors and local authorities, to provide doctors if necessary and notify next-of-kin if wished.

- In the event of serious illness or accident: Contact the hospital within twenty-four hours of notification; ask the Foreign and Commonwealth Office to contact next-of-kin; if the hospital is local, can visit within two days.

- In the event of death: Ask the Foreign and Commonwealth Office to contact next-of-kin, and liaise with sponsors about arrangements for the repatriation of the remains to the UK.

- Money difficulties: Advise on procedures for transferring money from the UK or elsewhere; contact friends/relatives/banks if other channels are unavailable; transfer money in emergencies.

- Repatriation: As a last resort arrange repatriation at public expense against an undertaking to repay.

Services the embassy/consulate is unable to provide
- Supply money for payment of bills.

- Obtain employment or accommodation for you.

- Offer legal advice, but will provide a list of local English-speaking lawyers.

- Intervene in commercial/labour disputes. (The commercial section can offer procedural advice on local commercial/business practices.)

- Investigate a crime.

- Give assistance if you hold dual British/Saudi nationality.

- Provide interpretation or translation services.

- Obtain entry or exit visas for Saudi Arabia.

CASE STUDY

Jim's contract is changed without notice

Jim, a doctor, accepted a staff position with a hospital in Saudi Arabia. The contract Jim signed is for a married status employee. Under the terms of the agreement, Jim's children's educational fees would be paid in full. Jim and his wife Jane have three children, Mark 17, Sara, 14 and Mary, 9. Mark was enrolled in a boarding school in England. Sara and Mary were enrolled in the local British school in Saudi Arabia.

After their first year in Saudi Arabia, Jim was notified that boarding school fees for children would no longer be paid to expatriate employees. Sara was now 15 and no longer allowed to continue her schooling in the Kingdom. By Saudi law all children can finish the school year in which they turn 15. After that they will have to continue their education outside the Kingdom or by correspondence.

When Jim signed his contact there was a clause allowing his employer to alter the terms of his contract without notice. Jim questioned his employer regarding this clause but was told changes rarely occur. Jim's contract is for three years and his employer will not release him from his contract.

Jim and Jane are now faced with paying university fees for Mark and unexpected boarding school fees for Sara.

DISCUSSION POINTS

You have been offered a lucrative contract to work in Saudi Arabia. Unfortunately, the contract is single status.

1. Will you and your family be able to cope with long (four-month) separations?

2. Will you and your family be able to accept that you may not be joining them for holidays, Christmas, anniversaries and birthdays?

3. Will you be able to cope with missing day-to-day family life?

6

Women's Issues

MAKING PRIMARY ADAPTATIONS

Getting around town

Western expatriate women coming to Saudi Arabia need to make many special adjustments in order to cope with the restrictions that are part of daily life in the Kingdom. First and foremost will be having to accept that you are not allowed to drive. This will affect every aspect of your daily life; from doing the shopping, getting the children to school, participating in activities, visiting the doctor, meeting friends and attending events outside your compound. Western women find it frustrating to be dependent on their husbands for transport. Western men often have difficulty adjusting to the extra burden this places on them; after a long day at work they may not want to go out again to do the shopping.

Some companies have drivers for the wives of senior employees, or these wives may share a driver on a rotation basis, but is is relatively rare. For women who share a car and driver it is advisable to set up a schedule in order to avoid any conflicts. Generally, women are dependent on the compound bus service, their husbands and taxis for their transport. Public bus (SAPTCO) transport is available in the major cities. Women must enter through the women's door and sit in the women's section of the bus, located at the back of the bus.

Organisation is the key!
Depending on taxis and the compound bus service means being organised! Compound buses follow a specific route, which may mean shopping for food one day and doing other errands on another day. Visiting friends, taking the children to the doctor, or going to shops off the compound bus route will require a taxi.

In organising your transport you must also take into consideration prayer time closing, as this affects when a taxi will be available. If you are trying to call a taxi, you will have to wait until after prayer time before they will answer the telephone. Also, take into account that all

Prayer Times

Tuesday, May 21

City	Fajr	Dhuhr	Asr	Maghrib	Isha
Makkah	4.13	12.17	3.33	6.55	8.25
Madinah	4.06	12.18	3.43	6.33	8.03
Riyadh	3.37	11.50	3.14	6.33	8.03
Dammam	3.18	11.36	3.05	6.33	7.53
Tabuk	4.05	12.30	4.03	7.21	7.51
Jizan	4.14	12.06	3.23	6.37	8.07

Fig. 11. Sample of prayer schedule which is published in the
English language newspapers daily.

shops close during prayer time, and shops are closed from the midday
prayer until 4 pm. In the evenings shops close for the Maghrib prayer
call before sunset, and for the Isha prayer call an hour after sunset.
Prayer call shop closings last for approximately thirty minutes.

Hiring a driver
You may wish to hire a driver for your personal use. Discuss this
with your sponsor/company as some companies employ a driver to
run errands and the driver may be able to provide some personal
transportation in addition to his regular duties. Alternatively, you
can contract with a taxi company for a driver to make scheduled
runs; for example, to take children to pre-school or activities. To
find a reliable taxi company, or a particular taxi driver, ask your
neighbours and friends whom they recommend. Your compound
may have a contract with a taxi company, which would ensure good
service. You can also negotiate with an individual taxi driver
directly; this may result in a cheaper price.

Taxi tips
- The recommended taxi to take is the white car with an orange
  stripe on each side.

- Never take a yellow taxi, these operate on a request stop basis
  and are not considered safe for women.

- Taxis do not have meters and fares can be quoted arbitrarily. Ask the fare price before you get into the taxi. You can often negotiate the price. If you are not sure what the fare is, ask a friend what she normally pays.

- Have the correct change; you are in a better position for price negotiations.

- Taxi drivers do not expect tips.

- Most drivers speak adequate English, but they may not know the routes.

- Always sit in the rear, right-hand seat where you can see the driver and give him instructions if he doesn't know the route.

Going out in public

The second major adjustment is having to ensure that you are properly dressed every time you leave your compound, or your private villa or apartment. As long as you follow the basic guidelines, and use good common sense and discretion, you will not run the risk of being criticised in public. *You must dress conservatively*: collar bone and elbows covered, skirts calf-length, no silhouette (long shirts worn over skirts or slacks to cover your bottom. Skirts and slacks should be loose fitting. An *abaya* may be worn over your street clothes.

Only in the city of Al Khobar may women go out in public without wearing an *abaya*, the voluminous black cloak worn by Arab women. Legally, Western women are not required to wear an *abaya*, but are encouraged to wear them. You should also carry a scarf in your bag in case you are told to cover your hair. Be particularly sensitive to the dress code during the holy month of *Ramadan*.

It is not a good idea to wear shorts under an *abaya*.

Parents are responsible for making sure their children are dressed appropriately in public, especially adolescent and teenage girls. Teenage boys should not wear shorts in public.

Clothing checklist
- Lightweight, natural fabrics are best for the intense heat.
- Loose outer clothing and cotton underwear are more comfortable in the heat.
- Bring some winter clothing and even rain gear. You will appreciate it, even though the winter season is quite short.

Dealing with criticism

During your stay in Saudi Arabia you will hear references to the *mutawwa'in mutawula* (plural). Originally known as the Committee for the Propagation of Virtue and Prevention of Vice, the *mutawwa* is a kind of moral volunteer force which may intervene to discourage, or discipline, people behaving inappropriately in public. Most frequently there are reports of women being told they are not properly dressed. If a woman is with her husband, they will always confront the man, because it is his responsibility to make sure his wife is properly dressed. They may also ask a couple for proof of marriage.

It is best to try to avoid any interaction with the *mutawwa*, but if you are approached always remain polite. You may discuss the incident with your Embassy afterwards.

Maintaining the right distance

Saudi Arabia is probably one of the safest countries in the world. Western women and children, however, usually attract a lot of stares, particularly when venturing into areas less frequented by other Westerners. It may make you feel uncomfortable, but nothing worse. It is, however, a good idea to maintain a polite but aloof attitude towards men in the streets and in the shops. Looking directly at men and smiling can be misconstrued. Should you receive any unwanted advances, make some *immediate verbal reaction*. Ignoring an advance is considered tantamount to approval.

Your children, particularly if they have fair hair, will attract a lot of attention, both from the Saudi women who find it a novelty and from the Asian men working in the Kingdom. Most of the Asian men are on single status contract and miss their own families.

LIVING WITH THE CLIMATE

If you arrive in the cooler months (November to March), acclimatising will not present a great problem. Throughout the Kingdom these months are relatively cool and pleasant, similar to British spring or summer weather. In Riyadh and other parts of the interior, it is quite cold at night. Bring some warm clothes. In other areas jumpers and light jackets are usually sufficient. There is rain, though amounts vary each year, so an umbrella and even wellingtons for the children can be useful.

Month	Mean temperature Celsius	Climate comments
Jeddah		
Jan	23.3	Usually hot and very humid
April	27.8	all year (90% humidity)
July	32.2	occasional rain in winter
Oct	28.9	
Dec	24.4	
Av annual temp	27.8	
Riyadh		
Jan	17.2	Very dry all year
April	29.4	Very hot April–Nov
July	38.3	Nights cold from Nov–March
Oct	30.0	Occasional rain or dust
Dec	20.0	storms in winter and spring
Av annual temp	26.1	
Dhahran		
Jan	15.6	Mostly dry with strong winds
April	25.6	and dust storms
July	36.1	from March–July
Oct	28.9	Humid Aug–Sept
Dec	17.8	Occasional rain Dec–April
Av. annual temp	26.7	

Fig. 12. Temperature and climate chart for some cities in Saudi Arabia.

By mid-April it is getting hot, and from May to the end of October daytime temperatures range between 33° and 45°C. In these temperatures it is best to avoid spending too much time outdoors during the day. In the central desert and in the Eastern Province, summer brings the *Shamal*, or north winds. The strong, hot wind will feel like a giant hairdryer. Occasionally there are dust storms which are similar to a thick fog. The dust can also creep into your home. Air conditioning makes life bearable during the hot months, but many people choose to leave the Kingdom for the entire school holidays to escape the heat.

Tips on beating the heat
- stay out of the midday sun
- wear a hat
- drink *lots* of fluids; if you feel thirsty you are already dehydrated
- wear sunscreen (SPF 8 – SPF 20, depending on skin type)
- dizziness, nausea and disorientation are danger signs.

WOMEN'S HEALTH MATTERS

Many women feel apprehensive when moving away from their family doctor and gynaecologist. There are numerous British and US trained doctors and gynaecologists working at hospitals and clinics within the Kingdom. The best advice for finding a doctor is to ask other women who they think is competent. The terms of your contract may require you to use a specific hospital or clinic for insurance purposes. If possible, ask the wives within your company what their experiences have been with medical care. Above all, don't let the prospect of having a baby in a foreign country alarm you. Saudi Arabia has a high birth rate and this is an area of medicine well catered for. Many expatriate women prefer to stay with their husbands and families to have their babies in the Kingdom, rather than face the turmoil of travel and separation during the last few months of pregnancy and the first few weeks after giving birth. (See Chapter 8, page 124.)

While waiting for the doctor
Women are generally asked to wait for the doctor in the ladies waiting room. It is advisable to bring your own reading material.

RUNNING YOUR HOME

Waiting for your shipment to arrive

The majority of living accommodation in Saudi Arabia is furnished. You will therefore not have to face camping in an empty house while you wait for your shipment to arrive. In many cases employees may be housed in temporary accommodation which is fully equipped, while they are looking for permanent housing and awaiting arrival of their shipment. For families the processing period of entry visas may mean that personal goods arrive in the Kingdom before the wife and children. If you are allowed a limited air shipment, here are a few suggested items:

- toiletries and make-up if you are fussy about brands
- extra supplies of prescription medicines (see Chapter 2, page 40 and Chapter 8, page 124)
- extra copies of passports and entry visas
- personal jewellery should be *hand carried* or left safely at home (insurance may not cover it in your shipment). You may prefer to leave things that cannot be replaced at home.

Acquiring furniture, appliances and electronics

Most accommodation will have appliances such as a fridge, cooker and washing machine. However, you will need to buy a television and VCR because European models do not work in the Kingdom. It is best to buy a multi-system TV and video recorder as many compounds have their own video libraries, but often the films available are recorded on different systems (European PAL, or US NTSC). Many compounds are wired with 110v. It is a good idea to take a voltage checker to test outlets. In the larger cities a good selection of electrical goods is available. Some electrical items, such as hairdryers and stereo equipment, are dual-voltage and can be switched for 110v or 220v. You may consider selling other items before you return to the UK. There is usually a good market for this type of goods.

Although accommodation is furnished, you may still want to buy items which will make your place more cosy. In the larger cities there is a wide range of household items available in both Western and more ethnic styles. Prices in the new shopping malls tend to be high. You can often find the same or equivalent goods in the older *suq* areas for much less.

HIRING HOUSEHOLD HELP

Part time household helpers

One of the perks of living in Saudi Arabia is that household help is easy to find and very affordable. If you are living on a compound, you may be approached by one of the maintenance staff who will offer to be your **house helper**. These men are usually from India, Pakistan, Bangladesh, Sri Lanka or the Philippines. The range of services offered by house helpers varies considerably. Some will clean the house, do windows, iron, babysit and (more rarely), cook and serve meals on special occasions. Within the small community of a compound, a house helper's reputation precedes him. If you are not approached and you want household help, ask your neighbours whom they recommend. The current rate (2000) for household help is SR 15–20 per hour. The babysitting fee is SR 25 per hour.

There are advantages to having a house helper who also works on the compound. He will know who to contact to have repairs taken care of quickly and who does the best work. Also, he will not have to check in with the gate guard to gain access to your villa. The authors have never heard of any cases in which a house helper has been accused, or suspected, of stealing.

Full time household helpers

It is also possible to hire full time maids, who will either live in or come in daily. If you plan to bring your maid, or employ a maid from outside the Kingdom, she will need a visa and *Iqama*. Your sponsor will make all the necessary arrangements required to bring your maid into the Kingdom. Because your sponsor/company obtains the visa and *Iqama* for your maid, your sponsor/company is responsible for your maid's activities. If she commits an illegal act, or damages any property, your sponsor/company is financially responsible. Her actions will also reflect upon you.

Salaries depend on the type of work, and previous experience, of the employee. Consequently salaries vary from SR 600 to SR 800 for maids from India, SR 800 (Indonesia), SR 800–1,000 (Philippines), prices vary according to sponsors. Some sponsors charge SR 1,200–2,000 per month Some household help can work half days for SR 800. Your maid is entitled to a thirty-day home leave every two years. As the employer, you are responsible for providing a return ticket to your maid's home country. If you plan to take your maid with you on your home leave you must get a letter of permission from your sponsor/company. Your sponsor/company will also have to arrange for an exit/re-entry visa for your maid.

If you are looking for full time help, but prefer not to have someone living in, ask your neighbours and friends for a recommendation. Word of mouth is very effective. There are many Eritrean and Filipino women already in the Kingdom who are interested in domestic work for Western families. Domestic helpers who come in daily are usually paid on an hourly basis, currently around SR 7–9 per hour. You may find it preferable to agree on a set number of hours per week and pay your employee on a monthly basis. You may have to pay for transport costs for a daily employee. (Note: Prices quoted are current for 2000.)

Working hours for full time domestic help

Obviously, a family employing someone on a live-in basis will have to work out a schedule with some flexibility, but the official regulations are as follows. The normal working week in Saudi Arabia consists of an eight-hour day, six days a week, or a forty-eight hour week. Friday is the day off, but many companies also require employees to work on Thursday mornings only. Employees are entitled to a rest period of one half-hour after five hours of continuous work. During the month of *Ramadan*, Muslim employees work only six hours a day, a thirty-six hour week. There are three official public holidays: *Eid al Fitr* (following the end of *Ramadan*), which lasts three days; *Eid al Adha* (during the month of pilgrimage, *Dhu'l Hijjah*) which lasts four days; and, the Saudi National Day on 23rd September.

Points to remember

- Ask around to get a good idea of what is the going rate of pay.

- Be clear about what the employee's duties and time off will be.

- You may have to negotiate overtime pay, but if you have set a limit, stick to it.

- Make sure your employee's *Iqama* is in order.

- It is best to have a written contract in order to avoid conflicts later.

LOCATING JOB OPPORTUNITIES

Unless you have been hired for a specific job and have your own

Iqama, wives accompanying their husbands will not be allowed to work outside their compounds. There are a few exceptions to this rule: schools, diplomatic offices and a few companies which have their offices located on a compound will hire women. These jobs are hard to come by and usually heard about through word of mouth.

Using your skills

Many women, however, find they can turn their skills into cottage industries. These services may be: hairdressing, specialised cooking, teaching aerobics, languages, musical instruments, or selling craft items. Volunteerism is another way to fill your days. The schools often seek volunteer help in the classrooms or libraries. There is also a wide variety of sports and social organisations which depend on volunteer help to run events and activities within the expatriate community.

Some successful home-based entrepreneurial activities
- hairdresser
- beautician
- reflexologist
- desktop publisher
- stained glass repairer
- travel agent.

Some activities available for women
- British Wives Association
- Intercultural Women's Association
- language classes
- computer classes
- craft classes and craft sales
- sports: tennis, squash, softball, bowling, aerobics.

This list just scratches the surface. For anyone with energy and enthusiasm the opportunities exist, it just takes time, energy and initiative to exploit them. It is a good idea to register with the nearest British Consulate or Trade Office when you arrive, as they can be a useful source of information on activities and organisations in your area.

Reasons why women enjoy living in Saudi Arabia
- Feeling safe on the streets and in shops.
- No worries of theft or physical harm.
- No home maintenance costs to worry about; everything included

in rental agreement.
- When the plumbing, or appliances break down they are repaired immediately.
- Without full time employment you have more time to be with your family.
- Time to take up a hobby.
- Time to develop a hobby into a lucrative business.
- Exposure to a new culture.
- Opportunity to meet people from different countries.
- Great opportunity to travel.

CASE STUDY

A wife has to change her travel plans

An American woman resident in Al Khobar was planning a visit back to the US. Since her husband could not take leave at that time she would be travelling from and returning to the Kingdom without him. She made her travel booking well ahead of time in order to secure a seat, as flights during that period were filling up. A few days before her scheduled departure, her husband applied for the necessary exit/re-entry visa for his wife. Luckily the company's Government Relations Officer happened to notice that the husband's *Iqama* was due to expire during the time his wife would be out of the Kingdom. All travel plans had to be postponed, and a new exit/re-entry visa issued quoting the husband's new *Iqama* number. Had he renewed his *Iqama* while his wife was out of the country, the number on her exit/re-entry visa would not have corresponded with the new *Iqama* number. She would have been refused entry to Saudi Arabia and would have had to go through the whole process of obtaining a new entry visa. Fortunately she was able to get on a flight home a few days later.

DISCUSSION POINTS

1. Are you flexible about changing your habits to accommodate new customs?

2. Are you self-motivated enough to accept challenges and turn them to your advantage?

3. Can you deal with gossip and clique politics in group situations?

4. Do you have an interest or hobby which you have always wanted to develop?

7

Shopping in Saudi Arabia

GETTING OUT AND ABOUT

Remembering the constraints

Shopping in Saudi Arabia is both fun and frustrating. Frustrating in the sense that as a Westerner you will have some constraints put upon you. They have been mentioned before in this book, but they bear repeating.

- Prayer time. Shops are closed for twenty to thirty minutes which mostly affects shopping in the early evening.

- Siesta time. Stores are also closed from approximately 11.30 am to 4 pm.

- *Ramadan*. During the holy month of *Ramadan* stores are open for a short period in the morning and then open from 8 pm until midnight.

Additional constraints for women
- Transport. Women can't run out to the trusty car and drive to the store. Most compounds provide a bus service to various shopping locations which is scheduled to meet the needs of the entire compound. This schedule may be inconvenient for you at times. On these occasions you will need to arrange for a taxi. Also, it is advisable to go out and about with another woman. If you are going out with a group, remember, only a man can sit in the front seat of a taxi with the driver.

- Proper dress. When you leave the compound dress very conservatively. Only in the city of Al Khobar may women go out without the *abaya*. In all other areas of the Kingdom an *abaya* is worn over street clothes. Carry a scarf with you in case you are told to cover your hair.

Planning and lots of time are the keys to an enjoyable shopping experience in Saudi Arabia.

Hint: When the call of nature strikes head for a hotel, restaurant, large department store or supermarket. Modern malls provide clean bathrooms. Always carry lots of tissue.

Locating shops and products

Because this book does not focus on one particular area within Saudi Arabia, store names, products and the merchandise mentioned can be found throughout the Kingdom. For specific stores, products, or shopping area locations within your area check the Further Reading section.

Throughout this chapter you will see the word *suq*. A *suq* is a market place. In Saudi Arabia many shops that sell the same merchandise are located next to each other. The carpet *suq* is where most of the carpet stores are located, the gold *suq* is where most of the gold stores are located. The women's *suq* sells merchandise geared for the running of the home such as kitchenware, fabric for clothing and sewing accessories. The majority of Western brand named stores, or stores selling merchandise from the West, are located in shopping malls. Shopping malls also include stores selling products from the Middle East and Asia. They offer a wonderful blend of East and West, where the shopper can browse in air conditioned comfort during the hot summer months. But the flavour of Saudi Arabia can only be found in the *suqs*.

The major shopping areas

There are three major shopping areas in Saudi Arabia.

- The city of Jeddah (also spelled Jiddah and Jidda) is located on the west coast.

- Riyadh, the capital of Saudi Arabia, is located in the middle of the country.

- Al Khobar is on the east coast. Dammam, also located on the east coast, and a few miles from Al Khobar, is the capital of the Eastern Province and has quite a lot to offer for shopping, but Al Khobar has taken over as *the* shopping city for the Eastern Province.

Many women who live in small towns or 'oil camps' travel to the major cities to do weekly shopping. For example, women living in

Yanbu travel to Jeddah, women living in Jubail or Ras Tanura to Al Khobar. For these women, their companies or compounds provide a bus which takes them to the nearest major city once a week.

Negotiating or bargaining

Bargaining is a time-honoured tradition in the Middle East. Many Westerners are put off by this practice. If you do not bargain for an item the shopkeeper will think you are not interested and will ignore you. Once you get the hang of it, you will begin to enjoy the experience. Relax, it's fun! Never think of bargaining as a test of wills. Always remain courteous and polite, never use rudeness or aggression as bargaining tools. Before you begin negotiations offer the customary greeting. Know the value of the item you are negotiating for: if you do not know the value, check at different stores to get a general idea of the price. Ask the clerk what the price is, then look shocked. Offer forty per cent less, now the clerk will look shocked.

As you barter back and forth and get close to your price, notice if the clerk's eyes travel to another assistant. You have just identified the owner or manager of the store. Now the real negotiations begin. Do not become impatient, bargaining should not be rushed. To get the price you want will take time. In some cases, when purchasing a carpet or expensive piece of jewellery, it is advisable to return to the store several times over a period of weeks. The owner is now aware that you are a serious customer. Remember, though, a good bargainer also knows when to leave. Each expat has developed his/her own technique for bargaining, and soon you will be sharing your secrets on how to get a great bargain. Remember, everything can be negotiated!

Sales

Merchandise goes on sale during the holy month of *Ramadan*. Once the assistant has given you the sale price, begin your negotiations with that price.

Buying food from supermarkets

In each major city there are at least two supermarket chains which have several locations within the city. Supermarkets are open seven days a week and only close for prayer time; they are open during the afternoon. Safeway is open twenty-four hours a day. Mastercard and Visa are accepted.

The supermarkets are clean and well stocked. You may not find the brand name you are used to but the product or a good substitute is always available. For example, real vanilla is banned because it contains alcohol, but imitation vanilla is available. Because there is a large international expatriate community in Saudi Arabia you will find speciality food items from all over the world.

- There is an excellent selection of fruit and vegetables. Locally grown produce is far cheaper than the imported varieties. There are greengrocers on practically every corner in residential areas.

- Fresh fish from the Gulf is excellent, a few to try are *hamour* (grouper), *hamra* (red snapper) and shrimp (prawns), to name a few. Salmon, sole, lobster, crab, *etc* are flown in fresh. There is also a wide selection in the frozen foods section.

- There is a wide selection of poultry to choose from: chicken (local and imported), turkey, duck, quail, pheasant and Cornish hens.

- The meat list is extensive: Dutch veal, Irish and American beef, Australian and New Zealand lamb, sausages, salamis and cold cuts. Absolutely no pork products are available.

- There is a fresh bakery along with packaged goods.

- Dairy products are made locally or imported. Do try some of the lovely Saudi cheeses.

- Ice cream, sorbet, sherbets and frozen ices are available.

- Frozen dinners, vegetables, entrées, breads, fish, poultry and desserts are well stocked.

- There is a wide selection of spices, nuts, coffee and tea sold in bulk or packaged. The bulk variety is fresh and can be purchased in the specific amount you require.

- Over the years the supermarkets have begun to stock some low fat, sugar free products but the list is meagre. You can purchase Nutrasweet, diet colas and sugar free preserves. There are a few low fat cake mixes and icings. Decaffeinated products are limited to coffee and tea.

- Pet food and products for your pets are available.

- Also available in supermarkets: toiletries, vitamins and minerals, cleaning equipment (mops, brooms, *etc*), kitchenware, baby items, some clothing, towels, bedding, light bulbs, electrical items, stationary, gift wrapping items, newspapers and magazines.

Safeway is located throughout the Kingdom. To compare prices between Britain and Saudi Arabia see Figure 13.

UK, Sainsbury's March, 2000		Safeway, Al Khobar, March 2000	
Bread, white family loaf	£0.59	Bread	£0.52
Butter, 500 g Lurpak	£1.86	Butter, Kerrygold, 454 g	£1.43
Margarine, 250 g Flora	£0.52	Margarine 500 g	£1.65
Milk, per litre	£0.49	Milk, 1 litre, 2 litre	£0.69/£1.21
Eggs, per dozen	£1.65	Eggs, doz	£0.43
Pork sausages, ½ kg	£1.59	Beef sausages per kilo	£4.86
Kelloggs cornflakes 750 g	£1.45	Kelloggs cornflakes 750 g	£2.42
Ariel soap powder, 1.2 kg	£2.39	Ariel, 3 kg box	£3.91
Fairy Liquid, 1 litre bottle	£1.65	Fairy Liquid, 1 litre bottle	£1.38
Homepride flour, 1.5 kg	£0.75	Local all purpose flour	£0.43
Heinz Baked Beans, 420 g	£0.31	Heinz Baked Beans, 420 g	£0.54
Minced beef, 1 kg	£2.98	Lean minced beef, per kg	£3.65
Tetley teabags, box of 80	£1.69	Lipton's 50 bags	£1.39
		Lipton's 200 bags	£4.51
Robertson's marmalade 340 g jar	£0.79	Robertson's marmalade 340 g jar	£1.47
Sugar, 1 kg bag	£0.45	Sugar, 1 kg bag	£0.48
Frozen peas, 1 kg bag	£1.19	Emborg frozen peas, 900 g	£2.04

Exchange rate: £1 = SR 5.75 confirmed by British Trade Office, Al Khobar, July 2000.

Fig. 13. Sample shopping basket comparing prices
UK/Saudi Arabia (July 2000)

Buying food from markets and smaller shops

Fruit, vegetable and fish markets
The vegetable and fruit *suqs* of Saudi Arabia are clean and fun to wander through. Produce is sold in bulk generally, so find someone who is willing to split the box with you. The *suqs* are far cheaper than the supermarkets and the produce is very fresh. Negotiating the price is required.

In many overseas locations it is necessary to sterilise fruits and vegetables for thirty minutes. This procedure is not necessary, simply use the normal cleaning and rinsing techniques you use at home.

Neighbourhood shops
Within every neighbourhood there is a street with small shops selling baked and canned goods. The selection is limited, but these stores are useful when you run out of basics.

Gourmet shops
Each city has a wonderful offering of shops that specialise in hard to find items. There are also speciality shops for pastries, cakes, breads, chocolates, cheeses, spices, fish, coffees and teas. The list continues to grow as more shops open.

Catering
For those occasions when you are entertaining a large group, hotels and restaurants provide full catering services at very reasonable prices.

SETTING UP YOUR HOME

Houseware
Houseware stores are as abundant as the merchandise they sell. Some items to look for include: bed and bath products, table linens, dishes, glassware, cutlery, small appliances (blenders, food processors, microwave and toaster ovens, irons). Saudi Arabia is a gourmet's delight, with all the gadgets and paraphernalia you could desire.

Hardware
Saco is a Kingdomwide chain stocking tools (for house and car), paint, hardware, houseware, electrical and plumbing supplies, cleaning products, curtain rods, ready-made picture frames or do-it-yourself kits, barbecues, gardening supplies, plants (real and artificial), outdoor furniture, sports equipment and camping equipment.

China and crystal
If you are shopping for china and crystal the name brands sold are: Waterford, Baccarat, Cristofle, Royal Doulton, Spode, Rosenthal,

Villeroy and Bosch, Heinrich, Wedgwood and many more. Do not look for bargains, but there are no taxes and your negotiating skills may net you a saving.

Furniture

Good quality American furniture is available through American Homes and Habitat. We have found the prices comparable to US ones. Savings are possible because no VAT taxes are charged.

Ikea sells Scandinavian furniture along with everything else you will need for your home. In Al Khobar the store is quite small and most items are ordered through the catalogue.

Rosewood furniture from Hong Kong, China and Pakistan is another good buy. Some shops will take custom orders. Rattan furniture from the Philippines is available with a wide selection to choose from.

Upholstery and curtains

Upholstery and custom-made curtains are inexpensive and both the material and the workmanship are excellent. There is a wide selection of material to choose from. Inquire whether the shop will accept your material or insist upon using their own fabric.

BUYING FOR THE FAMILY

Chemists

Each neighbourhood has its own chemist shop. In Saudi Arabia a chemist shop is called a pharmacy. Prescriptions are not required for antibiotics, antihistamines, birth control medications, hormone replacement therapy drugs, insulin, *etc*. Narcotics and several diet control drugs are not sold without a prescription. Antibiotics for children come in powder form which you have to mix yourself. Many of the over-the-counter remedies are sold in Saudi Arabia. Aspirin is difficult to find and is packaged in small amounts.

Learn the generic names of any medication you take. The brand name you are familiar with may not be sold in-Kingdom, whereas the generic name will help the pharmacist find the medication sold under a different brand name. If your doctor insists that you use a specific brand name medication, bring a supply with you, along with your prescription, in order to avoid problems with Customs when entering or exiting the country.

Along with prescription and non-prescription drugs, pharmacies carry a selection of toiletries, cosmetics, perfumes, sun lotion products, hair and nail care products and baby needs from formulas to disposable nappies.

Health stores
GNC is the main health store outlet in the Kingdom, offering a complete range of vitamins, minerals and food supplements. Herbal treatments, organic beauty treatments and cosmetics are also available.

Make up
Most major cosmetic companies are represented in the Kingdom. You may not find your brand in the first shop you try. Many shops are small and may carry only seven or eight brand names rather than the complete product line. Keep looking, it may be frustrating, but you will find it. The Body Shop, Crabtree and Evelyn, and the Reform Shop are represented in the Kingdom.

Perfumeries
Brand name perfumes can be purchased at cosmetic shops.

The Saudi perfume shops are well worth a visit. They sell fragrances in the form of concentrated oils known as the essence. Taif is famous for its roses and the perfume industry of Saudi Arabia will only use roses from this area. Many other oils are available and creating your own fragrance is a lot of fun. Incense, such as sandalwood, frankincense, myrrh and camphor can also be purchased in the perfume shops.

Buying clothing and shoes

Window shopping
In accordance with Islamic doctrines regarding images of the human body, shops are not allowed to use mannequins to display clothing. A few shops in the new shopping malls have introduced simplistic shapes in their display windows, mostly torsos, definitely no heads. Generally, window dressing in Saudi Arabia consists of a confusing array of items pinned or suspended on fishing line which fill the entire available space. Trying on clothes is officially not allowed. Some shopkeepers may let you use the broom cupboards, but you can always bring goods back with a receipt.

Sizes

Shops in Saudi Arabia sell clothing from all over the world. Each country has its own sizing standard. Consequently, shopping for clothes can be a bit confusing. Below are some sample clothing sizes from the major exporting countries to Saudi Arabia.

- Men's shirt sizes: US and UK size 16 = European and Arab size 41.

- Women's sizes: US size 10 = UK size 12, European size 38.

- Shoes: Women's sizes: US size 6 = UK size 4, European size 37.

- Men's sizes: US size 10–10½ = UK size 9, European size 43–44.

Shop assistants are adept at converting sizes.

Women's clothing

Many stores in Saudi Arabia offer quality clothing and new boutiques continue to open. Designer labels include: Max Mara, Mondi, Versace, Dior, Armani, Ferragamo, Escada and Laurel. Brand name stores located in the Kingdom are: Benetton, Sisley, Next, Liz Claiborne, Guess, BHS, Wrangler and Lee jean stores, with more brand name stores opening on almost a weekly basis.

Clothing in Saudi Arabia is expensive. Unless you are an average size you will have difficulty finding clothes to fit you properly. Generally, there are no fitting rooms in the stores. All shop assistants are male.

Personal items such as lingerie, panties, bras and tights are available, but in limited styles and sizes. Some women are uncomfortable purchasing personal items from male shop assistants.

Abaya shops

Saudi women are required to wear a black, full-length outer garment called an *abaya* over their street clothes when they appear in public. *Abaya* shops are located in the malls and *suqs*. Prices vary according to fabric and the amount of ornamental detail. Some *abayas* have intricate applique work or beautiful Palestinian embroidery. *Abaya* shops also sell gorgeous scarves in silk, cotton, polyester and blends. The scarves are quite large and can be used as shawls. They are a great buy!

Men's clothing

Just as there are many shops featuring women's clothing, there are an equal number that cater for men. Many men, though, feel the styles are a bit too *avant garde* for them. Men's clothing is also expensive.

Tailors

Both men and women have found that a tailor can be the solution to their clothing problems. Tailors are affordable and do excellent work. A good tailor is usually found by word of mouth. Many tailors will copy an outfit for you. Bring the item to be copied, or draw a sketch of it with your measurements. For a woman to be properly fitted she must go to a female tailor. Male tailors are not allowed to touch a woman.

Children's clothing

Jeddah, Riyadh and the Dhahran area have numerous new shopping malls which feature familiar names like BHS, Mothercare, Benetton. While it is comforting to shop in these stores, the prices are often uncomfortably high. For everyday play clothes and shoes the local *suqs* offer ample choice and very reasonable prices.

Shoes

There is a wonderful selection of shoes, if you have average size feet. Italian shoes dominate the market, but Bally is available. Clarks and Doc Marten shoes are also represented in-Kingdom. Children's shoes are sold in both shoe stores and children's clothing stores.

SHOPPING FOR FUN

Buying jewellery and watches

- Gold is definitely the best buy in Saudi Arabia. Jewellery is sold in 18 carats (Italian), 21 and 24 carats (Arabian and Indian). Gold is priced at the current rate per gram, with a small amount added on for design. Shop around as prices vary widely. Bargaining is a must.

- Gemstones and pearls are available in beautiful settings, but they are expensive.

- Silver jewellery is an excellent buy. There are many unique designs, in large and chunky styles or small and delicate pieces with intricate filigree work.

- Top-of-the-line watchmakers are represented in Saudi Arabia at prices that are substantially lower than England. Jewellery and watches can be purchased in the gold *suqs* and in shopping malls.

Hobbies and sports

Arts and crafts
Craft kits and art supplies can be found at Jarir's Bookstores, Ben Franklin's, Toyland and Toy Town.

Books, magazines and newspapers
The major bookstore chain in Saudi Arabia is Jarir's. They also sell greeting cards, stationery supplies, gift wrapping supplies, party supplies, children's games and videos, and a small selection of toys, picture frames and kits, artists' and drafting supplies. Supermarkets also have a good selection of newspapers and magazines. Before you buy a book, magazine, or hefty copy of *The Sunday Times* check for censorship. Pages will be torn out and pictures blacked out. Often the black ink will stain several pages. Books, magazines and foreign newspapers are expensive.

Books
There is a wide range of books available in English on subjects such as autobiographies, biographies, business, beauty, cooking, computers, health (medical textbooks and pharmacology), history, home decorating, gardening, infant and child care, travel. If the book is considered offensive to Islam it will not be available. There is an excellent selection of Middle East subjects such as history, culture, art, carpets, clothing, food and jewellery. Many of these books are 'coffee table' books with fabulous photographs. Unfortunately, they are also expensive.

Magazines
There is an excellent selection of news, computer and home decorating magazines in English, French and German languages. Fashion magazines are not available as the fashion photographs are considered offensive to Islam.

Newspapers
International newspapers, along with the leading newspapers from the world's major cities, are available.

CDs and audio tapes
There is a huge number of CD and tape stores. They sell the latest CDs and tapes, but they are expensive. If you are a woman, check to see if you are permitted in the store. For some unknown reason many CD shops do not allow women in. There will be a sign stating 'Ladies not allowed'.

Computers and software
PCs, laptops and notebooks are available, but they may not be the latest model on the market, and they are expensive. Software, on the other hand, is an excellent buy and the very latest programs are available. Generally, computers and software equipment are sold in the shopping malls. If you plan to take your computer back to the UK make sure it is compatible with the 220 voltage system.

Electronics
The latest home entertainment is available, from the big screen to the smallest screen, with or without stereo, from Walkman CD players to multiple CD players, from the simple 'boom box' to surround-stereo equipment. Televisions sold in Saudi Arabia are multi-system. The majority of electronics sold in-Kingdom are dual voltage, but do enquire if the voltage is 110, 220 or dual voltage if you want to bring them into the UK. Some equipment will be priced lower than in the UK, others will be much more. Your bargaining skills will also be a determining factor in the price. Electronics are located in the electronics *suq*.

Note on UK customs: Bringing electronics less than two years old into the UK can be very costly. Duty and VAT charges can add up to an additional twenty-six per cent over the purchase price of the item. The only exception is a change of residency to the UK.

Photographic equipment and processing
Many camera stores have one-hour film processing with very good results. There are a large number of camera stores in each city. Consequently, many stores have special discount days, or offer extra prints or rolls of film free. Photographic studios provide passport-size photo services. Some camera stores also offer this service. Camera shops are located in the electronics *suq* and the shopping malls.

Musical instruments
Yamaha pianos, synthesizers, brass instruments, drums and guitars

are available. Also of interest are the beautiful Arabic instruments. The single string guitar is named *rababah*, and the lute is *oud*. The pipes are named *mismah*.

Sewing
There is a wide selection of fabrics from the finest woollens to the most delicate lace, and haberdashery. Generally fabrics and sewing equipment are not sold in the same shop. Most fabric and sewing equipment will be found in the Women's *suq*. Prices are inexpensive.

Sports equipment
There is no one brand name store that is country-wide, but each city has several sports stores with a good selection of tennis gear (equipment, racket stringing, clothing and shoes) and workout clothes. There are a few speciality shops featuring golf and diving equipment. Sports stores are located both in the *suq* and shopping malls.

Camping and picnic equipment
Saco stores have a good selection of tents, coolers, folding chairs, barbecues, camp stoves, *etc*, for picnics and camping. The supermarkets have a smaller selection of coolers and outdoor furniture. Visit the tent *suq* for a custom-made tent, they are great for backyard entertaining or camping trips.

Toys
Toyland, Toys 'R' Us, Toy Town and the Early Learning Centre are the major toy shops in the Kingdom. Generally these shops are located next to a supermarket or in a shopping mall. There are many smaller toy shops located in the suqs. Along with toys there are model and craft kits, puzzles, tricycles, bicycles, playhouses, sandboxes, swing sets. Unfortunately, prices are expensive. If you prefer only quality toys, buy them on home leaves. The 10 Riyal shops are good for inexpensive toys and party-bag fillers for birthdays.

Buying Middle Eastern items
Walking through the *suqs* is a sensory experience. The wonderful fragrances from spices, coffees, perfumes and incense, the abundance of herbs, vegetables and fruits, the incredible colours of the carpets, the sparkle from brass and copper pots. All this makes for an experience only to be found in the Middle East.

Antiques

Antiques consist of: doors, windows, keys, carpets, weavings, Bedouin jewellery, clothing, veils, pottery, coffee pots, incense burners, kohl and henna boxes, swords and daggers (*khanjars*). Antiques are expensive, but many of these items are now being reproduced and, therefore, are quite affordable.

- Arab doors and windows are painted in bright colours with geometric patterns. Some doors are left in the natural wood and geometric patterns are burned on with an iron. Doors and windows of this design are no longer made and are therefore becoming rare as they are only found on old homes that are being torn down. Many doors and windows are displayed on walls. Another way of displaying them is to convert them to coffee or end tables covered with glass.

- Weavings are difficult to find, they come in bright oranges and reds. They are used for wall hangings. There are many excellent reproductions.

- Henna boxes are round boxes made of wood, and covered in leather and trimmed in brass. Henna (*hinna*) is a dye used on the hair. The dye is also applied to the hands and feet in intricate patterns for special occasions such as weddings.

- Kohl is kept in elaborate silver containers, most of which come from India. Kohl is a black powder made from the ashes of burnt almonds, benzoin and incense. It is used as eye make up and also protects the eyes from the harsh sun.

Carpets

Carpets can be either antique or new. The older the carpet, the more valuable. There are many different styles. Each style denotes the region, village, or city where the carpet was made. Persian carpets are fascinating to study, each carpet has a history and a story to tell. If you plan to buy a carpet, study first. There are numerous books on the subject. Also, visit various carpet shops, the shopkeepers enjoy talking about their merchandise. Many shopkeepers will allow you to take the carpet home for a few days before you purchase it.

Additional items

Additional items include: Syrian boxes made of inlaid wood and mother of pearl, table linens from Syria and Iraq. Palestinian embroidery, chests with carved wood or plated with brass, copper and brass pots, baskets, camel bags and saddles, and hubble bubble water pipes!

Art galleries
There are many excellent local artists represented through the numerous art galleries in the Kingdom. Many of the artists have allowed prints to be made of their work. The prints are quite reasonably priced. Most galleries offer framing services that are much cheaper than the UK.

Shopping malls
Many Middle East items can also be found in gift shops at the shopping malls. Art galleries and carpet stores are also located in the shopping malls. Due to the higher rent charged by the shopping malls goods tend to be more expensive than in the *suqs*.

CASE STUDY

A shopper finds learning Arabic numbers can save money
On a visit to a local market an Irish woman sees some of the traditional winter coats for sale. Since the stallholder is an Indian she asks him the price in English, although she can speak some Arabic. He quotes her SR 70, which she thinks is too expensive, and asks the price for some traditional-style waistcoats. He quotes her SR 60. She still thinks this is too high, and is still examining the garments when a Saudi couple walk up and ask the stallholder something in Arabic. The Indian holds up the small waistcoats and says *Talateen* or SR 30, exactly half the price he had quoted the Irish woman. When she reacts with shock, the Saudi man asks her in English what has happened. She explains, to which the Saudi replies, 'You never pay more than SR 25 for these'. She takes two waistcoats, hands the stallholder SR 50 and he accepts without protest.

DISCUSSION POINTS

1. Will the items you purchased be worth the additional shipping costs?

2. Will the items you purchased in Saudi Arabia blend with your decor at home?

3. Do you have space in your home for the items you purchased in Saudi Arabia?

8

Family Matters

Saudi Arabia can be a wonderful assignment for families, particularly those with young children. Compounds provide children with a safe environment where they can make friends quickly and enjoy activities such as roller-blading and riding bicycles, without the fear of the traffic. The expatriate community extends a warm welcome to newcomers, and helps them assimilate into their new surroundings. There are numerous social and sports activities to join. The best way to learn about these activities is to *ask your neighbour*; the 'jungle telegraph' is a very effective means of communication!

CHOOSING A SCHOOL

Saudi Arabia has its own education system where subjects are taught in Arabic according to Islamic principles. In the 1970s the Saudi Arabian International School (SAIS) was established to provide education for non-Muslim children throughout the Kingdom. Individual schools, registered for particular nationality groups, have been set up throughout the country. There are schools in Jeddah, Riyadh, Dhahran and Jubail, which follow the British curriculum. Elsewhere the international schools follow the American system.

Muslims must receive special permission from the Ministry of Education to attend a SAIS school (frequently the school itself can make these arrangements). There are Islamic schools (the Manarat Schools), which teach through the medium of English; these schools also prepare older students for various foreign examinations.

In 1997 the Saudi Arabian Government gave approval for non-Muslim students to continue their secondary education up to graduation level in the Kingdom of Saudi Arabia. Prior to that non-Muslim children could only attend school within the Kingdom through the academic year in which they turned 15. After the age of

15 they had to attend boarding school in the UK, Bahrain, or pursue their studies by correspondence. Several of the British and American schools throughout the Kingdom have now added classes so that children can complete the studies instead of having to go abroad. Check to see to what level of education the school you are interested in offers.

There is often pressure for places at the expatriate schools. Contact the school in the area where you will be living as soon as possible to secure entry for your children. Schools in Saudi Arabia often start very early in the morning 7.30 or 8 am, and usually finish between 1 and 3 pm, depending on individual schedules. Schools have a two- or three-week break at Christmas; they also have breaks for the Muslim holidays of *Eid al Fitr* and *Eid al Adha*. Below is a list of school addresses throughout the Kingdom.

Eastern Province
Abqaiq Academy (American). Tel: (03) 566 0410. Fax: (03) 566 2337.
British School, Dhahran Academy, PO Box 667, Al Khobar 31952. Tel: (03) 330 0555. Fax: (03) 330 2450.
Al Khobar British School, PO Box 4359, Al Khobar 31952. Tel: (03) 895 1404. Fax: (03) 894 2312. Ages 3–12.
Hafr Al Batin, 200 Villa, O&M Directorate, King Khalid Military City, PO Box 10023, Hafr Al Botin 31991. Tel: (03) 787 4234. Fax: (03) 787 4092.
Jubail British Academy, PO Box 10059, Madinat Al Jubail Al Sinaiyah 31961. Tel: (03) 341 7550. Fax: (03) 341 2808. Ages 4–13.
Jubail International. Tel: (03) 341 7550/7681. Fax: (03) 341 6990.
Rahima. Tel: (03) 846 4111. Fax: (03) 846 4222.

Jeddah
Continental School, PO Box 6453, Jeddah 21442. Tel: (02) 699 3936. Fax: (02) 699 1943. Now offers the International Baccalaureate.
Jeddah Preparatory School, British-Dutch Section, c/o British Consulate General, PO Box 6316, Jeddah 21442. Tel: (02) 654 2354. Fax: (02) 238 0232. Education up to IGCSE.

Western Province
Asir Academy (American). Tel: (07) 223 3961 ext 4086 or 4084. Fax: (07) 223 3961 ext 4083.
Asir Preparatory School, PO Box 34, Khamis Mushayt. Tel: (07) 222 0545 ext 3089. Fax: (07) 223 8991. Ages 5–11.
Taif. Tel: (02) 725 4888 ext 2285. Fax: (02) 725 4666 ext 2285.
Yanbu International. Tel: (04) 392 1088/9. Fax: (04) 392 1075.

Riyadh

British School Riyadh, PO Box 85769, Riyadh 11612. Tel: (01) 248 0386. Fax: (01) 248 0351.

The American School. Tel: (01) 491 4290 and the Multinational School. Tel: (01) 453 1686, now offer classes beyond age 15.

Boarding schools in Bahrain

St Christopher's School, PO Box 32052, Isa Town. Tel: (00 973) 685621. Offers GCSE subjects, O and A levels.

Bahrain International School, PO Box 934, Juffair, Bahrain. Tel: (00 973) 727828. (American system – British system has been discontinued.)

Points to remember
- Bring records of all your children's injections.
- Bring school records (reports, exam results, *etc*).

HEALTH CARE

For information on medical insurance benefits see Chapter 5, page 88. For information on women's health care concerns see Chapter 6, page 101. For information on prescription and over-the-counter drugs see Chapter 7, page 113.

Registering with and accessing the health care system

Once you and your family have been registered with your company's health care provider you will receive an **identification card** for each family member. Before the patient goes to the clinic they must have a form letter from your company. The form letter will have the name of the patient, and the reason for requesting care and a company stamp. In the case of an emergency a **letter of permission** is not required.

At the registration desk of the clinic the receptionist will ask for your identification card and letter of permission from your company. The receptionist will make up a file for you and direct you to the doctor or service you are requesting.

Modern medical care

Private hospitals/clinics offer the latest medical equipment. Doctors receive their medical training in England and the United States.

At the present time, many hospitals have signed agreements with university hospitals in the United States, allowing the Saudi facility access to medical information and consultations via satellite hookups.

Some of the specialised programmes available at many Saudi medical facilities include weight loss and exercise programmes, nutritional counselling, psychiatric counselling, plastic surgery and so on. There are also hospitals that specialise in a specific medical field, such as obstetrics, eye care, dental care.

ACS in Riyadh and Access in Al Khobar
Both of these organisations have a listing of psychologists and psychotherapists who are available to help expatriates and their children.

Health care concerns

Water
The water from house taps is safe to drink. Drinking water is referred to as sweet water. In some compounds water piped into the house is both sweet and regular water. Enquire if your house has both types of water and which taps have sweet water. Regular water is fine for cleaning and bathing.

During the hot summer months drink lots of water to prevent dehydration. If you are planning a family outing into the desert bring bottled water with you. Because no one knows when their car will break down, it is good idea to have bottled water in the car at all times.

Skin care
Many expats are unaccustomed to the hot sun of Saudi Arabia. When first exposing your skin to the sun, start with small amounts of time in the sun and avoid exposure between noon and 3 pm the hottest time of the day. Use a sun lotion with a high SPF level. Children's delicate skin, in particular, needs protection from the sun. Many areas of the Kingdom are very dry and this can have a damaging effect on the skin. Moisturising creams are a must.

Sunglasses
The most expensive sunglasses on the market are not necessary, but it is essential that the glasses have *both* UVA and UVB protection.

KEEPING BUSY AND HAVING FUN

Most compounds have swimming pools which become the focus of outdoor activities during the long, hot summer. Bring plenty of swimwear. Even 2- and 3-year olds quickly swim like fish with the daily exposure to the water. Pool toys are widely available in the Kingdom. Inevitably, though, the summer will also mean spending more time indoors because it is simply too hot to be outside for long. Think of it as a cold winter; plan this time for games, crafts, TV and videos.

Restaurants and food

There are many excellent international restaurants in the larger cities. Prices at restaurants in the major hotels tend to be quite high, though obviously the absence of alcoholic beverages will make a big difference to the bill. It is worthwhile exploring the numerous small and simple Middle Eastern, Thai, Filipino and Indian restaurants. The food is usually good and the prices very reasonable. They frequently offer take-away or home delivery service too. Most restaurants have a family section for couples and families, which is separate from the area reserved for single men. Western fast food restaurants, such as McDonald's and KFC, have spread throughout the Kingdom, but their prices are often higher than local-style restaurants.

Some Middle Eastern specialities to be experienced:

- *Shawarmas*, pitta bread sandwich filled with shredded lettuce, tomatoes, spices and chicken, beef or lamb roasted on a vertical grill. Usually cost SR 3–4.

- Cheese bread, Arab flat bread (*khobz*) baked with soft cheese and rolled up.

- *Labna zatar*, Arab flat bread baked with soft cream cheese and mixed herbs and rolled up.

- *Hummus*, dip made from chickpeas, parsley, garlic and tahini (like runny peanut butter made from sesame seeds), eaten with olive oil and Arab bread.

- *Tabouleh*, salad starter made from parsley, mint, cracked wheat and tomatoes.

Going on family outings

Saudi Arabia is very family-orientated in terms of entertainment. Along the coastal Corniche in Jeddah and Al Khobar there are numerous playgrounds which are popular in the cooler months with locals and expatriates alike. In the bigger cities there are outdoor amusement parks, and some of the large toy shops and shopping malls also have their own indoor mini-amusement parks, with rides and games for young people. Western fast food franchises frequently have adjoining play areas. These areas are very crowded at the weekends and in the evenings.

Major outdoor activities are confined to the cooler months. From November to March it is possible to enjoy the outdoors with trips to the desert for picnics, and camping trips. A favourite desert activity is collecting desert roses, which are crystallised barites. Snorkelling, diving and swimming can be enjoyed in some coastal areas. Men and young children can swim in the Red Sea and Arabian Gulf at public beaches. It is not possible for women or girls over the age of 12 to swim from public beaches due to the segregation of the sexes.

Joining organised activities

Children's activities
Wherever there are large concentrations of Western expatriates there are numerous organised activities for children. Soccer, softball, basketball, swimming and, more recently, roller hockey (with in-line skates) are all popular team sports. There are Scouts, Cubs and Girl Guide troops throughout the Kingdom. Information about these groups and activities is usually passed around via word of mouth. This is also the best way to find out about activities like ballet, piano and karate classes for your children. They are usually available, but are not widely advertised.

Adult activities
Adults also have sports activities such as soccer, softball, basketball, tennis, golf, riding and bowling. There are leagues set up for women as well as men. Many of the teams compete with teams throughout the Kingdom and the Middle East.

Women's groups organise fashion shows, lunches, card games, sports teams, arts and craft fairs, dances and tours. They offer classes in computers, languages, sewing, quilting, aerobics, arts and crafts and many more.

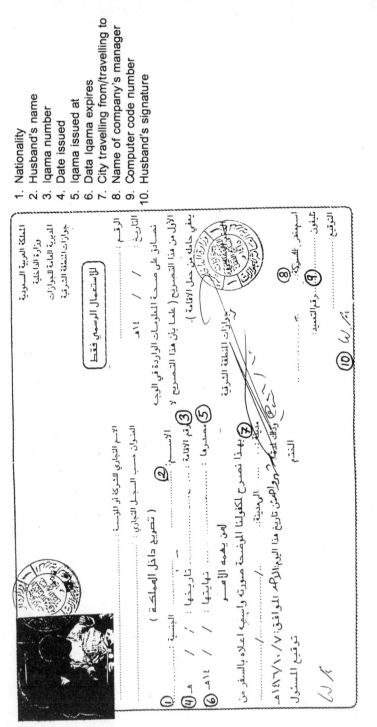

1. Nationality
2. Husband's name
3. Iqama number
4. Date issued
5. Iqama issued at
6. Data Iqama expires
7. City travelling from/travelling to
8. Name of company's manager
9. Computer code number
10. Husband's signature

Fig. 14. Travel permission document issued by Chamber of Commerce.

The British Businessmen's Association (BBA) is located in the major cities of the Kingdom.

The Travelling Naturalists have chapters throughout the Kingdom: in Riyadh they are called the Natural History Society. Along with guest speakers they also have treks into the desert and visit archaeological sites.

There are organisations throughout the Kingdom which bring in musical entertainment from Europe and the UK. Some of the larger compounds also provide musical entertainment with talent provided by the local expat community. Many compounds have amateur theatrical productions.

EXPLORING THE KINGDOM

There are several areas to visit within the Kingdom, and within your own province you will discover many places to explore. This section will whet your travel appetite by listing the better known areas of the Kingdom in a brief overview. For more in-depth information on travel within the Kingdom the local bookstores have an excellent selection of books.

Every major city in Saudi Arabia has an airport. Saudia Airlines has very good service linking all the major cities. Travel arrangements, including hotel and car rental, can be made through your travel agent. Many organisations have tours to the various cities throughout the Kingdom and they will make all the necessary arrangements for you. The major hotel chains offer package tours during the Islamic holidays. Travel agencies and hotels also advertise tours in the English language newspapers.

Obtaining a travel letter and letter of permission

Before you travel in-Kingdom you must have a **travel letter** from your company. Women travelling without their husbands also require a **letter of permission** from their spouses. A letter of permission is not required if you are travelling within the Province where you live.

Travelling in the desert

Each province has interesting desert areas to explore. Whether your excursion into the desert is for a day, or a camping trip for several days, there are a few basic safety precautions everyone must take.

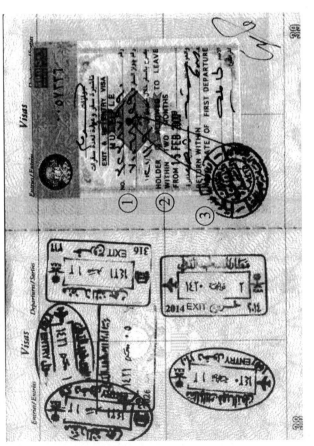

Fig. 15. Exit/re-entry visa.

1. Number
2. Date valid from
3. Period of validity (Hejira months)

- never go alone
- always tell someone where you will be going
- take plenty of water
- wear a hat
- take suntan lotion
- check your car for a spare tyre and the necessary tools to extricate the car from soft sand
- if your car breaks down, wait by it until help arrives
- *never leave your car.*

Exploring the Western Province

Jeddah area
See Chapter 3, page 55.

Red Sea
There are several resorts where your family can enjoy water sports, or just walking on the beach.

Taif
Located in the mountains, Taif is the city where many Saudis go to escape the hot summer season. Taif is famous for its beautiful roses. You can reach it by car or plane.

Exploring the Central Province

Riyadh area
See Chapter 3, page 59. Places to visit in Riyadh: Dira Square, the old walled city of Riyadh; Musmak Fortress; the Museum of Archaeology and Ethnography; Murabba Palace; Dir'yyah, the old ruined capital of the Al Saud; the Zoo; the Science Oasis, the hands-on exhibitions featuring astronomy, physics, mechanics and life sciences; the National Commission for Wildlife Conservation and Development (NCWCD) which has a wildlife exhibition and aquarium; the King Khalid Wildlife Research Centre which has a research and breeding programme for indigenous and endangered species of Saudi Arabia, reservations required.

Riyadh also has several parks to explore. Not to be missed: the camel races, which take place in the spring under the sponsorship of the National Guard. There is no betting. The horseracing track is located on Sitteen Street, with races on Sunday afternoons. There is no betting.

Exploring the Eastern Province

Half Moon Bay
A twenty-minute drive from Al Khobar. There is a public beach with picnic facilities and an amusement park. There is a large area for dune buggies, four-wheel drive vehicles and all-terrain vehicles; it's fun to watch the drivers tackle the dunes.

Hofuf
One of the oldest towns in Saudi Arabia. Places of interest are: the camel market; *Suq Al Khamis* (Thursday market), located near the Agriculture and Irrigation Ministry building, off King Abdul Aziz Street, has everything! The Covered Market, which covers several blocks from Share'a al-Khabbaz street to the Municipal Circle. The Covered Market is even larger than the Al Khamis Market! Pottery caves are located a short distance outside Hofuf.

   The caves of Jebel Al Qarah are located six miles east of Hofuf and are a popular weekend destination. Many of the springs have been blocked off for swimming. The Al Qarah caves are a two-hour drive from Al Khobar.

Qatif
Also spelled Katif, a one-hour drive from Al Khobar. The Thursday market resembles an old fashioned flea market. There is a wonderful fruit, vegetable and fish market. Don't forget to negotiate!

Tarut
The island of Tarut is connected to the mainland by the causeway from Qatif. Tarut Castle is an old fort built by the Portuguese in 1521. Now basically in ruins, it is still fun to visit.

Bahrain
The Island Emirate of Bahrain is accessible via the King Fahd Causeway. Bahrain offers excellent shopping, restaurants, hotels, beach resorts, the National Museum, the Portuguese Fort and the Tree of Life. You will need an exit/re-entry visa, your car registration and a travel letter from your company. Women travelling without their husbands will need a letter of permission.

TRAVELLING FROM SAUDI ARABIA

All airports located in the major cities are serviced by international carriers. The majority of international flights depart between 11 pm and 2 am. Tickets can be purchased through a travel agency or directly from the airline ticket office. Discounted tickets are available, but if paying with a credit card there will be a three per cent service charge. Many travel agencies will tell you they only accept cash for discounted tickets. Insist on credit card payment, they do accept them.

Most travel agencies do not sell package tours, but they can arrange for accommodation, car rental, international driver's licence (for men only – must have a Saudi driver's licence) and Eurail passes.

Travelling from Saudi Arabia is relatively easy. You will need the following documents: passport, exit/re-entry visa, travel letter and, for a woman, a letter of permission to travel from husband. There is a departure tax of SR 50 at the airports.

DISCUSSION POINTS

1. Have you considered the impact of an international move on your child's education?

2. Have you considered the impact on your pet, and your wallet, of a six-month quarantine upon your return to the UK?

3. List five ways an international posting could benefit your family.

Further Information about Arabic

EVERYDAY ARABIC EXPRESSIONS

Arabic is quite a difficult language to master, partly because of its complex grammar and partly because of the tremendous differences between regional dialects. Classical Arabic, the written language as preserved intact in the *Qur'an*, can be understood throughout the Arab world but it is seldom used in everyday speech. Expatriates living in Saudi Arabia often have little opportunity to speak Arabic since they may have little social contact with the local population. English is widely used for business purposes. Most of the shop attendants and workmen are from a variety of Asian countries and, again, English is a common language. If you are keen to explore off the beaten track, however, a little Arabic is very useful. The Saudis and other Arabs are generally delighted if you try to speak their language. The following are some useful words and phrases.

Greetings

Hello	*As salaam 'alaykum* (literally: peace be upon you)
Response	*Wa 'alaykum salaam* (and upon you peace)
Hello (informal)	*Marhaba*
Response	*Marhabtayn*
Good morning	*Sabah al khayr* (morning of fortune)
Response	*Sabah al noor* (morning of light)
Good evening	*Mesaa al khayr*
Response	*Mesaa al noor*
Welcome	*Ahlan wa sahlan*
Response	*Wa bikum*

General conversation

How are you? (to a male)	*Kayf haalak*

(to a female)	*Kayf haalik*
(to a group)	*Kayf haalkum*
Positive reponse: fine/good/ fortunate	*Tayyib/kwayyis/bi khayr* (all followed by *al Hamdulila*)
Thanks be to God	*al Hamdulila*
God willing	*Insh'allah*
Please (formal) (to a male)	*Min fudlak*
(to a female)	*Min fudlik*
(to a group)	*Min fudlikum*
Please (used colloquially)	*Mumkin* (literally: possibly)
Thank you	*Shukran*
Response	*Afwan* (don't mention it)
No matter	*Ma'laysh*
How much is this?	*Bikam hatha*
Yes	*Na'am* or (colloquial) *ai-wa*
No	*La*

Miscellaneous terms

Tribal (or nowadays business) leader	*Sheikh*
Prince or governor	*Amir*
King	*Malek*
Kingdom of Saudi Arabia	*Mamleka al Arabeeya Al Saudia*
Manager	*Moodir*

Arabic numbers

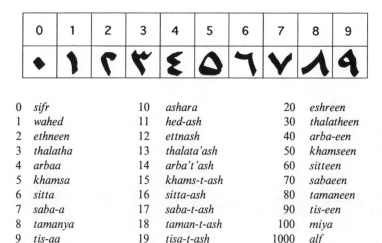

0	1	2	3	4	5	6	7	8	9

0	*sifr*	10	*ashara*	20	*eshreen*
1	*wahed*	11	*hed-ash*	30	*thalatheen*
2	*ethneen*	12	*ettnash*	40	*arba-een*
3	*thalatha*	13	*thalata'ash*	50	*khamseen*
4	*arbaa*	14	*arba't'ash*	60	*sitteen*
5	*khamsa*	15	*khams-t-ash*	70	*sabaeen*
6	*sitta*	16	*sitta-ash*	80	*tamaneen*
7	*saba-a*	17	*saba-t-ash*	90	*tis-een*
8	*tamanya*	18	*taman-t-ash*	100	*miya*
9	*tis-aa*	19	*tisa-t-ash*	1000	*alf*

Numbers above 20 appear as follows:

  21: *wahed-wa-eshreen* (one and twenty)
  35: *khamsa-wa-thalateen* (five and thirty)
101: *wahed-wa-miya* (one and hundred).

Since Arabic script is different from English it is rendered phonetically and there are variations according to regional dialects. The 'kh' in Arabic is pronounced like the 'ch' in the Scottish word 'loch'. Arabic is written from right to left but numbers are written left to right.

Useful Addresses

EMBASSIES AND CONSULATES

The British Embassy, PO Box 94351, Riyadh 11693. Tel: (01) 488
0077/488 0088. Fax: (01) 488 2373.

The British Consulate GeneralTel: (02) 654 1811. Fax: (02) 654 4917.

The British Trade Office. Tel: (03) 882 5300. Fax: (03) 882 5384.

The Royal Embassy of Saudi Arabia, 30 Charles Street, London
W1X 7PM. Tel: (020) 7917 3000.

Consular Section: as above.

Economic Section: 127 Sloane Street, London SW1. Tel: (020)
7730 8657.

Commercial Section: 15 Queen's Street, London W1X 7PM. Tel:
(020) 7917 7441.

Health Office: 119 Harley Street, London W1N 1DH. Tel: (020)
7935 9931.

GOVERNMENT ORGANISATIONS AND AGENCIES

Saudi Arabia Ministries

Ministry of Commerce, PO Box 1774, Airport Rd, Riyadh 11162.
Tel: (01) 401 2220/4708. Fax: (01) 403 8421.

Ministry of Communications, Airport Rd, Riyadh 11178. Tel: (01)
404 2928/3000. Fax: (01) 403 1401.

Ministry of Finance & Economy, Airport Rd, Riyadh 11177. Tel:
(01) 405 0000/0080. Fax: (01) 405 9202.

Ministry of Foreign Affairs, Airport Rd, Riyadh 11124. Tel: (01) 406
7777/6836. Fax: (01) 403 0159.

Ministry of Health, Airport Rd, Riyadh 11176. Tel: (01) 401 2220/
2392. Fax: (01) 402 9876.

Ministry of Information, Nassiriya Street, Riyadh 11161. Tel: (01)
401 4440/3440. Fax: (01) 402 3570.

Ministry of Interior, PO Box 2933, Airport Rd, Riyadh 11134. Tel:
(01) 401 1944. Fax: (01) 403 1185.

Ministry of Justice, University Street, Riyadh 11137. Tel: (01) 405 7777/5399.

Ministry of Labour and Social Affairs, Omar bin Al-Khattab St, Riyadh 11157. Tel: (01) 477 1480/478 7166. Fax: (01) 477 7336.

Ministry of Petroleum and Mineral Resources, PO Box 757, Airport Rd, Riyadh 11189. Tel: (01) 478 1661/1133.

Ministry of Post, Telegraph and Telephone, Intercontinental Road, Riyadh 11112. Tel: (01) 463 7225. Fax: (01) 405 2310.

Minstry of Public Works and Housing, Washm St, Riyadh 11151. Tel: (01) 402 2268/2036. Fax: (public works) (01) 402 2723; (housing) (01) 406 7376.

Saudi Arabia agencies

Central Department of Statistics, Off Airport Rd, Behind Ministry of Finance Bldg, Riyadh 11187. Tel: (01) 405 9638/401 4528. Fax: (01) 405 9493.

Customs Department, PO Box 3483, Riyadh 11471. Tel: (01) 401 3334. Fax: (01) 404 3412.

Directorate General of Zakat and Income Tax, Off Airport Rd, Behind Ministry of Finance Bldg, Riyadh 11187. Tel: (01) 401 0182/404 1537. Fax: (01) 404 1495.

Department of Commercial Registration Agencies Section Ministry of Commerce, PO Box 1774, Riyadh 11162. Tel: (01) 401 2220/ 401 4708. Fax: (01) 403 8421.

General Organisation for Social Insurance (GOSI), PO Box 2963, Riyadh 11461. Tel: (01) 478 5721/477 7735. Fax: (01) 477 9958.

Jeddah Seaport (Jeddah Islamic Port), Jeddah 21188. Tel: (02) 643 2552.

Dammam Seaport, PO Box 28062 (King Abdulaziz Seaport), Dammam 31188. Tel: (03) 833 2500. Fax: (03) 857 9223.

Chambers of Commerce and Industry

The Saudi Council of Chambers of Commerce and Industry, PO Box 16683, Riyadh 11474. Tel: (01) 405 3200/405 7502. Fax: (01) 402 4747.

Eastern Province, PO Box 719, Dammam 31421. Tel: (03) 857 1111. Fax: (03) 857 0607.

Jeddah: King Khalid St, Ghurfa Bldg., PO Box 9549, Jeddah 21423. Tel: (02) 651 5111, (02) 651 0996.

Riyadh: Dhahab St, PO Box 596, Riyadh 11421. Tel: (01) 404 0044/
0300/402 2700. Fax: (01) 402 1103.
PO Box 567, Tabuk. Tel: (04) 422 2736/0464. Fax: (04) 422 7378.
Taif: Al Sadad St, Wadi Widj, PO Box 1005 Taif. Tel: (02) 736 4624/
3025. Fax: (04) 738 0040.
Yanbu: King Abdulaziz Street, PO Box 58, Yanbu. Tel: (04) 322
4257/322 4258. Fax: (04) 322 6800.

United Kingdom
Arab-British Chamber of Commerce, 6 Belgrave Square, London
SW1X 8H. Tel: (020) 7235 4363. Fax: (020) 7245 6688.
Committee for Middle East Trade (COMET), 33 Bury Street,
London SW1Y 6AX. Tel: (020) 7839 1170/1191. Fax: (020) 7839
3717.
Confederation of British Industry (CBI), Centre Point, 103 New
Oxford Street, London WC1A 1DU. Tel: (020) 7379 7400. Fax:
(020) 7240 1578.
Energy Industries Council, Newcombe House, 45 Notting Hill Gate,
London W11 3LQ. Tel: (020) 7221 2043. Fax: (020) 7221 8813.
London Chamber of Commerce and Industry, Middle East and
North Africa Section, 33 Queen Street, London EC4R 1AP. Tel:
(020) 7248 4444. Fax: (020) 7489 0391.
The Middle East Association, Bury House, 33 Bury Street, London
SW1Y 6AX. Tel: (020) 7839 2137. Fax: (020) 7839 6121.
Saudi Arabian Airlines, Atlas House, 173 Victoria St, London
SW1E 5NA. Tel: (020) 7629 8803.
Saudi Arabian Information Centre, Cavendish House, 18 Cavendish
Square, London W1M 0AQ. Tel: (020) 8995 7777.

Department of Trade and Industry
Overseas Trade Services, Kingsgate House, 66–74 Victoria Street,
London SW1E 6SW. Tel: (020) 7215 5000. Fax: (020) 7215 4831.

DTI Regional Offices (Government Offices):
Government Office for London, Bridge Place, 157/161 Millbank,
London SW1P 4RW. Tel: (020) 7217 3221. Fax: (020) 7217 3450.
For Eastern Region, Building A, Westbrook Centre, Milton Rd,
Cambridge CB4 1YG. Tel: (01223) 346700. Fax: (01223) 346701.
For East Midlands, The Belgrave Centre, Stanley Place, Talbot St,
Nottingham NG1 5GG. Tel: (0115) 971 9971. Fax: (0115) 971
2404.

For South East (Guildford Area), Bridge House, 1 Walnut Tree Close, Guildford, Surrey GU1 4GA. Tel: (01483) 882255.

For South East (Reigate Area Office), Douglas House, London Road, Reigate RH2 9PY. Tel: (01737) 226900.

For South West (Plymouth Office), Mast House, Shepherds Wharf, 24 Sutton Road, Plymouth, Devon PL4 0HJ. Tel: (01752) 635000. Fax: (01752) 227647.

For the North East, Eastgate House, King's Manor, Newcastle upon Tyne NE1 6PA. Tel: (0191) 201 3300. Fax: (0191) 202 3744.

For the North West, Sunley Tower, Piccadilly Plaza, Manchester M1 4BA. Tel: (0161) 832 9111. Fax: (0161) 952 4099.

For Yorkshire and Humberside, 25 Queen Street, Leeds LS1 2TW. Tel: (01133) 280 0600. Fax: (01133) 233 8301.

For West Midlands, 77 Paradise Circus, Queensway, Birmingham B1 2DT. Tel: (0121) 212 5000. Fax: (0121) 212 1010.

The following also act as DTI Regional Offices:
Scottish Trade International, 120 Bothwell Street, Glasgow G2 7JP. Tel: (0141) 228 2633. Fax: (0141) 221 3712.

Welsh Office Industry Department, New Crown Building, Cathays Park, Cardiff CF1 3NQ. Tel: (029) 2082 5111.

Industrial Development Board – Export Unit, IDB House, 64 Chichester Street, Belfast BT1 4JX. Tel: (028) 9023 3233. Fax: (028) 9023 1328.

Other organisations associated with the DTI
DTI Export Control Organisation, 6th Floor, Kingsgate House, 66–74 Victoria Street, London SW1E 6SW. Tel: (020) 7215 5404. Fax: (020) 7215 4231.

Export Market Research Scheme, ABCC, 4 Westwood House, Westwood Business Park, Coventry CV4 8HS. Tel: (024) 7669 4484. Fax: (024) 7669 5884.

Export Market Information Centre, 1st Floor, Kingsgate House, 66–74 Victoria Street, London SW1 6SW. Tel: (020) 7215 5444. Fax: (020) 7215 4231.

Prelink Ltd, Communications Building, 48 Leicester Square, London WC2H 7LT. TEl: (020) 8900 1313. Fax: (020) 8900 1268. (Export intelligence – subscription service.)

Other government departments which offer help
Ministry of Agriculture, Fisheries and Food. Tel: (020) 7270 8080. (Now an automated answering system: dial this number, then

choose relevant option.)

Defence Export Services Organisation (DESO), MOD. Tel: (020) 7218 9000. Fax: (020) 7807 8207.

Department of Education. Tel: (020) 7925 5000. Fax: (020) 7925 6931.

Department of the Environment. Tel: (020) 7890 3000 (as for MAFF).

Department of Health. Tel: (020) 7210 3000 ext 5956. Fax: (020) 7210 5820.

Department of Transport. Tel: (020) 7276 3000 ext 5228. Fax: (020) 7276 5216.

EDUCATIONAL/CULTURAL ORGANISATIONS

UK

The Anglo-Arab Association, 21 Collingham Road, London SW5 0NU. Tel: (020) 7373 8414. Fax: (020) 7373 2077. Same address for Council of Advancement of Arab-British Understanding, and Saudi British Society.

The British Council, 10 Spring Gardens, London SW1A 2BN. Tel: (020) 7930 8466. Fax: (020) 7389 6347. The British Council also has a CD ROM available giving extensive information on Arabic and Islamic related research currently in progress in the UK.

British Society for Middle Eastern Studies (BRISMES), Faculty of Oriental Studies.

Islamic Texts Society, 22a Brooklands Avenue, Cambridge CB2 2BB. Tel: (01223) 335106. (Purpose: to increase understanding of Island in the West.)

Establishments offering Islamic or related studies in the UK

University of Leeds, (Arabic Studies), Leeds, West Yorkshire LS2 9JT. Tel: (0113) 233 3421. Fax: (0113) 233 3420.

School of Oriental and African Studies, (Islamic Societies and Cultures), Thornhaugh Street, Russell Square, London WC1H 0XG. Tel: (020) 7637 2338. Fax: (020) 7436 3844.

University of Durham, (Islamic Studies with a Middle Eastern Language), Old Shire Hall, Durham DH1 3HP. Tel: (0191) 374 2000. Fax: (0191) 374 3740.

University of Edinburgh, (Studies in Islamic Art), Secretary's Office, Old College, South Bridge, Edinburgh. Tel: (0131) 650 1000. Fax: (0131) 650 2147.

University of Manchester, (Islamic and Jewish Studies), Oxford

Road, Manchester M13 9PL. Tel: (0160) 275 2000. Fax: (0161) 275 2407.

University of Oxford, (Arabic with Islamic Studies and History). University Offices, Wellington Square, Oxford, Oxfordshire OX1 2JD. Tel: (01865) 270000. Fax: (01865) 270708

University of Birmingham, Newman College, (PgDip in Islam), Genners Lane, Bartley Green, Birmingham, West Midlands B32 3NT. Tel: (0121) 476 1181. Fax: (0121) 476 1196.

Schools

Eastern Province

Al Khobar British School, PO Box 4359, Al Khobar 31952. Tel: (03) 882 5303

Abqaiq Academy (American). Tel: (03) 566 0410. Fax: (03) 566 2337.

British School, Dhahran Academy, PO Box 667, Al Khobar 31952. Tel: (03) 330 0555. Fax: (03) 330 0555 ext. 2037.

Hafr Al Batin Academy, 200 Villa O&M Directorate, King Khalid Military City, PO Box 10023, Hafr Al Batin 31991. Tel: (03) 787 4234. Fax: (03) 787 4092.

Jubail British Academy, PO Box 10059, Madinat Al Jubail Al Sinaiyah 31961. Tel: (03) 341 7550. Fax: (03) 341 6990.

Jubail International. Tel: (03) 341 7550, (03) 341 7681. Fax: (03) 341 6990.

Jeddah

Continental School, PO Box 6453, Jeddah 21442. Tel: (02) 699 3936, Fax: (02) 699 1943.

Jeddah Preparatory School, British–Dutch Section, c/o British Consulate General, PO Box 6316, Jeddah 21442. Tel: (02) 654 2354. Fax: (02) 238 0232.

Western Province

Asir Academy, (American). Tel: (07) 223 3961 ext 4086 or 4804. Fax: (07) 223 3961 ext 4083.

Asir Preparatory School, PO Box 34, Khamis Mushayt. Tel: (07) 222 0545 ext 3089. Fax: (07) 223 8991.

Taif. Tel: (02) 725 4888 ext 2285. Fax: (02) 725 4666 ext 2285.

Yanbu International. Tel: (04) 392 1089, (04) 392 1088. Fax: (04) 392 1075.

Riyadh
British School Riyadh, PO Box 85769, Riyadh 11612. Tel: (01) 248 2387/0386. Fax: (01) 248 0351.
American School. Tel: (01) 491 4290.
Multinational School. Tel: (01) 453 1686.

Boarding schools in Bahrain
St Christopher's School, PO Box 32052, Isa Town. Tel: (00 973) 685621.

TRANSLATING SERVICES

Saudi Arabia
Dr Ahmed Audhali, Law Firm, Attorneys, Counsellors and Translators, PO Box 1158, Al Khobar 31952. Tel: (03) 864 3011/864 3793/899 1655. Fax: (03) 894 5837.
Dr Mohamed H. Hoshan, PO Box 2626, Riyadh 11461. Tel: (01) 464 8363. Fax: (01) 463 2083. Commerce and company laws. Translation services available.

UK
All Languages Limited, Nelson House, 362–364 Old Street, London EC1V 9LT. Tel: (020) 7739 6641. Fax: (020) 7739 6542.
Central Translations Limited, 2/3 Woodstock Street, London W1R 1HD. Tel: (020) 7499 7370. Fax: (020) 7409 2774.
Marguet and Ball Translations, 45 Endwell Road, London SE4 2NE. Tel: (020) 7732 1741. Fax: (020) 7358 9214.

BANKS AND INVESTMENT

UK
J. Henry Schroder Wagg & Co, 120 Cheapside, London EC2B 6DS. Tel: (020) 7658 6000. Fax: (020) 7658 3950.
Al Rajhi Investment Corp Ltd, Berkeley Square House, Berkeley Square, London W1X 5LA. Tel: (020) 7409 1770. Fax: (020) 7493 0933.
The Saudi British Bank, 18c Curzon St, London W1Y 8AA. Tel: (020) 7409 2567. Fax: (020) 7495 2329.

Saudi Arabia
Head offices
National Commercial Bank, PO Box 3555, Jeddah 21481. Tel: (02)

649 3333.

Al Bank Al Saudi Fransi, PO Box 7888, Jeddah 21472. Tel: (02) 404 2222.

Al Bank Al Saudi Hollandi, PO Box 6677, Jeddah 21452. Tel: (02) 406 7888/401 0288.

Riyadh Bank Ltd, head office and Jeddah branch, PO Box 1047, Jeddah 21431. Tel: (02) 647 4777.

Saudi American Bank, PO Box 490, Jeddah 21411. Tel: (02) 653 3555.

Saudi British Bank, head office: Riyadh, PO Box 9084, Riyadh 11413. Tel: (01) 651 2121.

PUBLISHERS AND PERIODICALS

BBC World Service, PO Box 76, Bush House, Strand, London WC2B 4PH. Tel: (020) 7240 3456. Fax: (020) 7240 4899.

Saudi Arabia

Arab News, PO Box 4556, Jeddah 21433. Tel: (02) 639 1888/639 3223. Riyadh office: (01) 441 9933.

Riyadh Daily, PO Box 851, Riyadh 11421. Tel: (01) 487 1000. Fax: (01) 479 4048.

Saudi Gazette, PO Box 5576, Jeddah 21432. Tel: (02) 667 4020/667 4408. Riyadh office: (01) 465 3324.

UK Ltd, The British Embassy, PO Box 94351, Riyadh 11693. Tel: (01) 488 0077. Fax: (01) 488 2373. Official British Government magazine for business and commerce in Saudi Arabia.

UK

DTI Export Publications, PO Box 55, Stratford-upon-Avon, Warwickshire CV37 9GE. Tel: (01789) 296 212. Fax: (01789) 299 096.

The Middle East and North Africa, Europa Publications, 18 Bedford Square, London WC1B 3JN. Tel: (020) 7580 8236. Fax: (020) 7637 0922.

H H Saudi Research and Marketing, Arab Press House, 184 High Holborn, London WC1V 7AP. Tel: (020) 7831 8181. Fax: (020) 8831 4051.

Saudi Press Agency, 18 Cavendish Square, London W1. Tel: (020) 7495 0418.

Stacey International, 128 Kensington Church Street, London W8

4BH. Tel: (020) 7221 7166. Fax: (020) 7792 9288. Publishes a wide range of books about Saudi Arabia.

GENERAL BUSINESS/COMMERCE

UK
British Offset Office, Ministry of Defence, Castlewood House, 77–91 New Oxford Street, London WC1A 1DS. Tel: (020) 7829 8514. Fax: (020) 7829 8116.

Saudi Arabia
British Offset Office, UK Ministry of Defence, PO Box 1003, Riyadh 11431, Saudi Arabia. Tel: (01) 419 5957. Fax: (01) 419 8469.

Dhahran Int. Exhibition Co, The Eastern Region, Dammam. Tel: (03) 833 7900.

Riyadh Exhibitions Co Ltd, Riyadh. Tel: (01) 454 0637.

Petromin, PO Box 757, Riyadh 11189. Tel: (01) 478 1328.

Saudi Industrial Export Co, Representative Office, 4 Stanhope Gate, London W1Y 5LA. Tel: (020) 7491 4016. Fax: (020) 7491 4027.

LEGAL CONTACTS

Saudi Arabia

Eastern Province
Dr Ahmed A. Audhali, Law Firm, Attorneys, Counsellors and Translators, PO Box 1158, Al Khobar 31952. Tel: (03) 864 3011/ 864 3793/899 1655. Fax: (03) 894 5837.

Mr Jubai Hadi Al Massaid, Al Masoud Legal Consultants, PO Box 1552, Al Khobar 31952. Tel: (03) 895 2836. Fax: (03) 895 2093. A law firm handling cases in court, and dealing with commercial, bank and labour disputes.

Ismail S. Nazer, PO Box 154, Al Khobar 31952. Tel: (03) 833 0590. Fax: (03) 833 1075. Lawyers to Saudi Aramco.

Riyadh
Law Firm of Salah Hejailan, Al Ihsa Street, PO Box 1454, Riyadh 11431. Tel: (01) 479 2200. Fax: (01) 479 1717. Legal adviser to Her Majesty's Ambassador. Specialises in law of commerce, banking, shipping, joint ventures. Translation in connection with legal work undertaken by the firm. **Criminal and family work not**

undertaken.

Dr Mohamed H. Hoshan, PO Box 2626, Riyadh 11461. Tel: (01) 464 8363. Fax: (01) 463 2083. Commerce and company laws. Translation services available.

Abdul Aziz A al Mohaimeed, PO Box 16545, Riyadh 11474. Tel: (01) 405 3274. Fax: (01) 402 9549. Commercial and labour disputes and contract law, civil rights, tax and social insurance matters.

Jeddah

Salah Al Hejailan, 11th floor Alireza Towers, PO Box 15141, Jeddah 21444. Tel: (02) 653 4422/651 2413. Fax: (02) 651 7241.

Nader Law Offices, 19 Abuzinadah Street, PO Box 3595, Jeddah 21481. Tel: (02) 665 2067. Fax: (02) 660 8709.

Al Amana Office for Debt Collection and Settlement of Commercial Disputes, Suite 203 Kaki Commercial Centre, PO Box 587, Jeddah 21421. Tel: (02) 665 6375. Fax: (02) 669 2681.

UK

Fox and Gibbons, 2 Old Burlington Street, London W1X 2QA. Tel: (020) 7439 8271. Fax: (020) 7734 8843.

Clifford Chance, Blackfriars House, 14 Bridge Street, London EC4V 6BY. Tel: (020) 7282 7000. contact: Michael Dark. (Associated with Salah Hejailan, Riyadh.)

Jones Day Reavis and Pogue, Bucklersbury House, 3 Queen Victoria Street, London EC4N 8NA. Tel: (020) 7236 3939. Fax: (020) 7236 1113.

Nader Law Offices (head office Jeddah), 41 Redcliffe Close, 276 Old Brompton Road, London SW5 9HY. Tel: (020) 7373 0975. Fax: (020) 7835 2251.

Trowers and Hamlins, Sceptre Court, 140 Tower Hill, London EC3N 4JQ.Tel: (020) 7423 8000. Fax: (020) 7423 8001.

Nabarro Nathanson, 50 Stratton Street, London W1X 6NX. Tel: (020) 7493 9933. Fax: (020) 7629 7900.

Further Reading

TRAVEL AND GENERAL

Arab Gulf States, Gordon Robison (Lonely Planet, 1993). Well researched manual on travel throughout the Arabian Peninsula. His section on Saudi Arabia gives a good potted history of the country.

Arabian Sands, Wilfred Thesiger (Motivate Publishing, Dubai, 1994). Classic account of his travels through the Empty Quarter with the Bedouin in the 1940s. Gives good insight into Bedouin culture and values.

Aramco and its World, ed. Ismail I. Nawwab, Peter C. Speers and Paul F. Hoye, 1981.

Berlitz Saudi Arabia (Berlitz Pocket Guides, 1993).

Campsites of the Riyadh Region, Mark Guile (self-published, 1995). Available in the Kingdom from Jarir Bookstores.

Desert Tracks from Jeddah, Patricia Barbor (Stacey International, 1996).

Desert Tracks from Riyadh, Ionis Thompson (Stacey International, 1995).

Desert, Marsh and Mountain, Wilfred Thesiger (Motivate Publishing, 1979, 1994).

In the Footsteps of the Camel, Eleanor Nicholson (Stacey International, 1983). American family's encounters with Bedouin Tribes of the Eastern Province in the 1950s.

Jeddah Old and New (Stacey International, revised edition 1996).

The Kingdom of Saudi Arabia, ed. William Facey (Stacey International, 9th edition 1993). Well illustrated coffee table book showing overall view of the Kingdom.

The Marsh Arabs, Wilfred Thesiger (Motivate Publishing, 1994). Travels among the Marsh Arabs of Iraq.

Riyadh Handbook, Ionis Thompson (Stacey International, 1996). Practical everyday guide to living in Riyadh. A *Jeddah Handbook* is also planned.

Red Sea Reef Fishes, Dr John Randall (Inmel, 1992).

Red Sea Safety: Guide to Dangerous Marine Animals, Dr Peter Vine (Inmel, 1994).

The Seven Pillars of Wisdom, T. E. Lawrence (Cape, London, 1935).

The Story of the Eastern Province of Saudi Arabia, William Facey (Stacey International, 1994).

Travels in Arabia Deserta, Charles Doughty (London, Cape/Medici Society, 1921). Fascinating account of travels in the Arabian peninsula by the 19th century British traveller.

Saudi Arabian Handbook (Knight Communications Ltd, 1997).

Saudi Arabia, all you need to know, Dr Nasser Ibrahim Rashid, Dr Esber Ibrahim Shaheen (International Institute of Technology, USA, 1995). Exhaustive portrait of the Kingdom and its people; includes many useful statistics and an extensive Arabic glossary.

Undiscovered Asir, Thierry Mauger (Stacey International, 1993).

SOCIAL AND POLITICAL

Arabia, Johnathan Raban (Picador, 1987). Though somewhat dated and omitting Saudi Arabia, still an excellent portrait of the Gulf countries and insight into Arab attitudes.

The Arabs, Peter Mansfield (Penguin Books, 3rd edition 1992). Social and political survey of the Arab world from pre-Islamic times.

The Arab Gulf and the Arab World, ed. B. R. Pridham (Croom Helm, 1988).

Desert Warrior, HRH General Khaled Bin Sultan with Patrick Seale (HarperCollins, 1995). Personal view of the Gulf War by the joint forces commander.

A History of the Arab Peoples, Albert Hourani (Faber & Faber, 1992).

The Kingdom, Robert Lacey (Hutchinson, 1981). Well researched outline of the historical development of present day Saudi Arabia and the House of Saud.

The Making of Saudi Arabia 1916-1936 from Chieftaincy to Monarchical State, Joseph Kostiner (Oxford University Press, 1993).

Passion and Politics, Sandra Mackey (Penguin, 1992, 1994). Excellent analysis of historical background to Western–Arab relations.

The Saudis, inside the Desert Kingdom, Sandra Mackey (Harrap, 1987). Extensive portrayal and analysis of the political and social structure of the Kingdom.

The Times Guide to the Middle East, eds Peter Sluglett and Marion Farouk-Sluglett (The Times Books, 1996).

The Turbulent Gulf, People, Politics and Power, Liesl Graz (I. B. Tauris & Co Ltd, London & New York, published in association with the Gulf Centre for Strategic Studies).

CULTURAL

At the Drop of a Veil, Marianne Alireza (Houghton Mifflin, 1971). An American woman who married into a prominent Jeddah family gives a close-up portrait of Saudi women's life in Jeddah in the late 1940s.

At Home in the Fourth Dimenson, Merriam Mattar (Inmel Publishing, London, 1994). Arab family life from a Western woman's viewpoint.

Familiarity Breeds Content, Kathy Cuddihy (Peregrine Publishing, Riyadh, 1995).

Islam and Christian Muslim Relations (Carfax Publishing Company, PO Box 25, Abingdon, Oxfordshire OX14 3UE).

Islamic Quarterly (Islamic Cultural Centre & London Central Mosque, 146 Park Road, London NW8 7RG).

Saudi Customs and Etiquette, Kathy Cuddihy (Peregrine Publishing, Riyadh 1990).

Traditional Crafts of Saudi Arabia, John Topham *et al* (Stacey International, 1982).

Women of Arabia, Marianne Alireza (*National Geographic*, October 1987).

BUSINESS

Arab-British Trade, Arab-British Chamber of Commerce, Business Information Dept, 6 Belgrave Square, London SW1X 8PH. Tel: (020) 7235 4363. Fax: (020) 7235 1748. Monthly journal.

Arab World Agribusiness, Fanar Publishing WLL, PO Box 10131, 8th floor, Bahrain Tower, Manama, Bahrain. Tel: (00 973) 213900. Fax: (00 973) 211765. In the UK from Jeremy Wright, Ramblers, Ludgores Lane, Danbury, Nr Chelmsford, Essex CM3 4JW. Tel: (01245) 223969. Fax: (01245) 226835.

Businessman's Guide to Saudi Arabia, Chamber of Commerce & Industry for the Eastern Province, PO Box 719, Dammam 31421.

Doing Business in Saudi Arabia, Whinney Murray & Co, PO Box 2732 Riyadh, Saudi Arabia 11461.

Gulf Construction & Saudi Arabia Review, Hilal International (UK) Ltd, Crescent Court, 102 Victor Road, Teddington, Middlesex TW11 8SS.

Gulf Marketing Review, EMAP Business International Ltd, Meed House, 21 John Street, London WC1N 2BP. Analysis and monitoring of marketing techniques and consumer trends in Gulf countries.

The Merchants, Michael Field (The Overlook Press, New York, 1985). Now dated, but still very informative look at the big business families of Saudi Arabia and the Gulf States.

The Economist Business Traveller's Guides, Arabian Peninsula, The Economist Publications, London (Prentice Hall, New York).

MEED, Middle East Business Weekly, EMAP Business International Ltd, Meed House, 21 John Street, London WC1N 2BP.

The Middle East, IC Publications Ltd, 7 Coldbath Square, London EC1R 4LQ. Business and current affairs.

The Middle East Broadcast & Satellite, ICOM Publications Ltd, Chancery House, St Nicholas Way, Sutton, Surrey SM1 1JB. News market reports for broadcast professionals in the Middle East.

Middle East Communications, ICOM Publications Ltd, Chancery House, St Nicholas Way, Sutton, Surrey SM1 1JB.

Middle East Economic Digest, EMAP Business International Ltd, Meed House, 21 John Street, London WC1N 2BP.

Middle East Electricity, Reed Business Publishing, Quadrant House, The Quadrant, Sutton, Surrey SM2 5AS.

Middle East Expatriate, Hilal International (UK) Ltd, Crescent Court, 102 Victor Road, Teddington, Middlesex TW11 8SS. Articles on expatriate life in the Gulf and financial advice for expatriates.

Middle East Finance Guide, EMAP Business International Ltd, Meed House, 21 John Street, London WC1N 2BP.

Middle East Gulf Directory, UK Advertising, Ramblers, Ludgores Lane, Danbury, Chelmsford, Essex CM3 4JW. *Yellow Pages* for the Gulf States.

The Middle East Review, Walden Publishing Ltd, 2 Market Street, Saffron Walden, Essex CB10 1HZ. Economic and political profiles.

Saudi Arabia, a Meed practical guide, ed. Edmund O'Sullivan (*Middle East Economic Digest*, 21 John Street, London WC1N 2BP).

Saudi Business, Arab News Bldg, off Sharafia, PO Box 4556, Jeddah 21441. Tel: (02) 653 4753.

Saudi Commerce & Economic Review, Eastern Province Chamber of Commerce, PO Box 719, Dammam 31421. Tel: (03) 857 1111 ext 4053. Fax: (03) 857 0607.

Saudi Economic Survey, PO Box 1989, Jeddah 21441. Tel/fax: (02) 642 8245. Weekly.

Saudi Arabian Financial Markets, Shaik Ahmed Banafe (self-published, 1993). Available from Jarir Bookstores in the Kingdom.

Working in the Gulf, Dr Hamid Atiyyah (International Venture Handbooks, 1994). An expatriate's guide to the employment law of the Gulf Arab States.

Internet resources

http://www.arab.net, Extensive information resource on doing business in Saudi Arabia and other Arab countries.

http://www.saudinf.com, more than 2000 pages of information on every aspect of the Kingdom of Saudi Arabia.

http://www.webcrawler.com, *Select/trav/mideast.html*, Travel, social and cultural information covering countries of the Middle East.

http://www.yahoo.com/regional/countries/Saudi_Arabia, Travel, social and cultural information covering countries of the Middle East.

CD-ROM

GCC Business Database CD-ROM, available from ALISSA @ EMIRATES.NET.AE, or by fax from any of the following numbers: (996) 3 834 3673 (Al Khobar), (966) 1 477 7906 (Riyadh), (966) 2 683 5752 (Jeddah), (973) 291601 (Bahrain), (971) 4 699672 (Dubai).

International Link, International Printers and Publishers, Inc, 8027 Leesburg Pike, Suite 209, Vienna, Virginia 22182, USA.

Index

153